DOES JESUS
LIKE CAKE?

Text copyright © Susanna Spanring 2003
Illustrations copyright © Ann Kronheimer 2003
The author asserts the moral right
to be identified as the author of this work

Published by
The Bible Reading Fellowship
First Floor, Elsfield Hall
15–17 Elsfield Way, Oxford OX2 8FG
ISBN 1 84101 319 6

First published 2003
10 9 8 7 6 5 4 3 2 1 0

Acknowledgments
Unless otherwise stated, scripture quotations are taken from the Contemporary English Version
© American Bible Society 1991, 1992, 1995. Used by permission/Anglicizations © British and Foreign Bible Society 1997.

Scripture quotations taken from the *Holy Bible, New International Version*, copyright © 1973, 1978, 1984
by International Bible Society. Used by permission of Hodder & Stoughton Limited. All rights reserved.
'NIV' is a registered trademark of International Bible Society. UK trademark number 1448790.

A catalogue record for this book is available from the British Library

Printed and bound in Malta

DOES JESUS LIKE CAKE?

(and other recipes for life)

SUSANNA SPANRING

Thank you...

To my husband, Paul, who supplied endless ideas, inspiration, meals, childcare and computing assistance while I was working on this book; to my three children, who never cease to delight and astonish me; and to my own parents, for all their love and support and for the wonderful childhood they gave me, which I was able to plunder for these stories.

CONTENTS

FOREWORD

This book has so many good points I find it difficult to begin.

Perhaps the most important message it contains is wisdom—the wisdom of Jesus Christ, the wisdom we need to live a practical Christian life in the times we are living in.

The book contains some challenging 'recipes for life' and also some great recipes for those of you possessed of a sweet tooth!

It is a book which can be used at home, enabling parents to guide the family into the teaching of Jesus whilst having lots of fun together, and it can be just as useful to primary school and Sunday school teachers, providing solid grounding for those who want to lead children on to a better way of life, living out the love of Jesus.

In this book you will learn how to be a Christian of love and joy, which is the example Jesus set before us.

I cannot recommend this book too highly. It is a truly lovely book.

Sir James Galway OBE

INTRODUCTION

Does God care about Jasmin the Dustbin when she is the victim of the school bullies? Can a little blue stone really bring good luck? What happens if a class full of donkeys all want to play Mary in the school play? And why is home-grown broccoli more prickly than the supermarket kind?

In this book, three children, Andy, Robby and Anna, find out all kinds of things about these and other knotty problems. Together with Jim, a chef, they discover not only different delicious recipes to bake, but also 'Recipes for life'. These recipes, which come from the Bible, help them to make sense of—and cope with—their own everyday experiences.

This book is intended for use both as a family storybook and as teaching material for primary education and church-based groups. Each chapter contains a Bible passage linked thematically to a story, a recipe, a group discussion and an activity (a game to play or something to make, sometimes a song to sing), and ends with a prayer.

The 'teaspoon prayer', which comes at the end of every chapter, is part of the recipe theme running through the book. Recipes often call for one teaspoon of salt, cinnamon or other flavourings. This is a very small amount, but it changes the taste of the finished product. In the same way, prayers don't need to be long or full of difficult words, but if we talk to God a bit every day, it changes the flavour of our whole life. The abbreviation for teaspoon (tsp) is used to divide prayers into Thank you, Sorry and Please.

All Bible references are from the Contemporary English Version.

All measurements and oven temperatures are metric.

Chapter 1

AN EGGSPLOSIVE EXPERIENCE

> 'The Son of Man came to look for and to save people who are lost.'
>
> LUKE 19:10

This is the first story about three children, Andy, Robby and Anna. Before you read about them, maybe you should get to know them a bit. Andy is the eldest and he has brown hair and blue eyes. He likes fishing and hates tidying up his room. Robby is in the middle. He is rather quiet with reddish hair, freckles and green eyes. He spends hours in the garden on his own with his collection of sticks. Both the boys would love to play computer games every day, but unfortunately their mum is rather strict about such things and limits them to weekends only. Anna is the youngest. She has two blonde plaits and

makes a big fuss every day about the tangles being combed out of her hair. She loves to draw and is always creating things out of bits of rubbish.

In this story the children get to know the new lodger who lives downstairs and make a few interesting discoveries about both cakes and life.

The parents of Andy, Robby and Anna were both musicians and often had to work late at night. They tried to avoid working on the same evening, but every so often there was a clash and they both had to be away. Whenever that happened, out would come the tattered list of potential babysitters. At the top of the list, written in Mum's neat handwriting, stood the words 'Possible Victims' and she would spend hours on the phone ringing one friend after another. It always took her ages to find someone who was willing and able to come.

One day, during breakfast, the phone rang. Mum went to answer it and came back beaming.

'That was a very old friend,' she announced to the children as they munched their cornflakes. 'He's moving back into this area and looking for somewhere to live. I told him that he could have the room downstairs as a bedsit, and live with us.'

Three pairs of jaws stopped their rhythmic crunching and opened in horror.

'We don't want anyone living down there!' cried Robby. 'Where will we put the bikes?'

'And my doll's pram and the footballs. And there are loads of spiders down there,' said Anna.

'We'll find somewhere for all that junk,' said Mum firmly, her eyes shining. 'Just think! No more hassle when Dad and I both have to be out. We'll have a permanent babysitter. And he's ever so nice. I know you'll like him.'

But the children were not at all pleased with this idea. Even if this person happened to be an old friend of Mum and Dad, they didn't want him living downstairs.

'Why can't I look after the others, Mum?' said Andy. 'After all, I'm nearly eleven.'

'And I'm five and Robby's nine,' chimed in Anna.

'Yes, we're not babies any more. We can manage. And you won't be away that often,' added Robby, hopefully.

But the arrangement was made and that was how, four weeks later, Mum was able to sit playing her cello at an evening concert, knowing that her children were safe and sound at home with an old friend she could really trust. His name was Jim.

Jim was rather plump. His huge, brown eyes were so bright and lively that they almost seemed to be lit up by some unknown source. But Anna, Robby and Andy were determined not to like him. Violent hammering, interesting snatches of music and delicious smells floating up the stairs from his flat were hard to ignore, but the children

had already decided. Jim was most definitely not wanted, and that was final. On the evening when his official duties as babysitter (how they hated that word!) began, they held a whispered council of war.

'We'll show him that we can cope on our own,' said Andy.

'Yes. And to show him we don't really want him, we'll hardly speak to him,' agreed Robby.

'Only the most important things, like "Please pass the biscuits",' added Anna thoughtfully.

At that moment, Jim came into the kitchen. Three unfriendly faces glowered at him. He took one look and flung up his arms in self-defence.

'OK, OK! If looks could kill, I'd be drawing my last breath now. Mercy! Have mercy!' Anna's face twitched. She wanted to laugh. He did look so funny. But Andy kicked her under the table, and quickly she rearranged her mouth in a thin, disapproving line.

'Tomorrow it's our mum's birthday,' announced Andy, 'and we want to make her something.'

'That's a good idea,' said Jim.

'A surprise,' said Andy. 'We can manage on our own.'

'Well...' said Jim, hesitating a little. 'Tell you what. I'll just pop downstairs and make myself a cup of coffee, and if you need me, you can come and get me.'

He plodded down the stairs and opened his new front door. It didn't quite feel like home yet. He brewed himself a nice cup of coffee and was just flopping on to his old sofa when the picture he had hung on the wall only an hour ago suddenly shuddered violently as a loud bang echoed through the house. It sounded like a gunshot. Another explosion was followed by bloodcurdling screams and then two more loud shots. Jim's coffee cup landed on his new carpet as he raced out of his front door and up the stairs to the flat above, where the noise was coming from.

He burst in and stopped, his heart beating fast. He was looking straight into the kitchen, where beneath a wooden table the three children were cowering, all looking very pale.

'What's going on?' asked Jim, staring at their frightened faces. 'Is everything all right?'

Andy emerged from under the table.

'We were just making a cake for our mum,' he said, 'when suddenly, there was this almighty explosion.'

'It was like shooting on the telly,' said Anna, crawling out to join her brother. She was trembling. Robby suddenly pointed dramatically with his finger.

'Oh no!' he cried. 'Look at the microwave!'

The inside of the microwave, which was lit up with the fan still humming, was covered in little pearls of a yellow substance and seemed to contain a good deal of steam.

Anna began to cry.

'Everything's going wrong,' she sobbed. 'We just wanted to warm up the eggs a little in the microwave. They were so cold, straight from the fridge, and Andy said for a cake they had to be at room temperature. Now all we've made is a huge mess! Mum's going to be so angry when she gets home.'

There was a short silence while the children waited for Jim to be cross with them. But his brown face creased up into a delighted, shiny grin and he began to laugh.

'Didn't you know that if you microwave eggs in their shells they explode?' he chuckled. 'I'm a chef, but I've never, ever tried out that recipe. I always wanted to see for myself what would happen and now I know. What an incredible noise they make when they burst open! I thought there was someone robbing a bank up here. But don't worry. I'll help you clear up.'

The mess was unbelievable. Anna had dropped a whole bag of flour in her fright, and Robby had somehow managed to tread in the butter. But Jim worked fast and efficiently and organized hot chocolate for everyone as well. And as they hoovered, dusted, scrubbed, scraped and sipped hot chocolate together, Andy, Robby, Anna and Jim all began to be friends.

'Did you say you were a chef?' asked Andy, some time later, after a good deal of tidying-up had taken place.

Jim nodded.

'Oh, couldn't you help us make another cake for our mum?' pleaded Anna.

'It's no good,' said Robby gloomily. 'We haven't got any more eggs.'

'How many eggs do you need?' asked Jim. 'What did your recipe say?'

'We didn't actually have a recipe,' said Andy sheepishly. 'We thought it might be fun to make up our own.'

'No recipe?' said Jim. 'Well, there's always more chance of success if you follow a recipe. It's got to be a good one, mind. Believe me, I've experienced some terrible ones in my time. But I've got the very thing—a cheesecake. It's very easy to make and it's delicious. Your mum will love it. Hang on a sec!'

He ran out of the room and clattered down the stairs. When he came back, he was carrying a large book in one hand and a basket in the other. The book looked much used and was battered and stained with countless coffee rings.

'Is that your recipe book?' asked Anna, with awe.

He laughed. 'I have got two large boxes filled to bursting with different recipe books. But I haven't unpacked them yet and I'm not going to start now. No, this is my Bible and I just brought it up because last Sunday at church, a friend of mine gave me a great recipe and I stuck it in here for safe keeping.' Then he paused for a moment, his head on one side.

'But in a way, this is a recipe book,' he said thoughtfully, opening the Bible and flicking through the pages. The children could see that it was filled not only with small black print, but also with multi-coloured underlinings and various remarks written in scrawling handwriting. 'It's got recipes for life. Cooking without a recipe can be pretty disastrous, but it's nothing in comparison to living life without a good recipe to follow. God's word, the Bible, has the very best ones.'

As he spoke, Jim was still leafing through his Bible. At last, not finding what he was searching for, he picked the book up by the covers and shook it. A snowstorm of scruffy, scrawly bits of paper fluttered to the floor and Jim pounced on one.

'Here we are!' he said triumphantly. 'I knew that recipe was in there somewhere.' He then lowered his voice as though this was a very important moment.

'Moist golden cheesecake,' he said, and there was something about the way he said it that made all the children's mouths begin to water.

'Strong men have wept for a morsel of this,' he added, rummaging around in his basket and pulling out a bag of sugar, a box of eggs and some tubs of cream cheese. 'I hope your mum likes cheesecake.'

So the children were able to make something for Mum's birthday after all. And the cake was so delicious that their mother had to share more of it than she might have chosen, had it been left up to her.

Moist golden cheesecake

(Quick, easy and delicious)

★ 1kg low-fat cream cheese (fromage frais or quark)
★ 300g sugar
★ 4 eggs
★ 8 dessertspoons semolina
★ 2 heaped teaspoons baking powder

1. Put all ingredients into a roomy bowl and mix thoroughly, using an electric mixer.

2. Pour mixture into a greased and floured 26cm round cake tin.

3. Bake at 180°C for one hour.

Serve with whipped cream flavoured with a few drops of vanilla essence and one tablespoon of sugar.

FAILED RECIPE? THE MASTER CHEF CAN HELP

 Danger! Cooking an unopened, raw egg in the microwave really is disastrous. Do not try it.

You need:
- ☆ A glossy recipe book with mouth-watering illustrations
- ☆ A bowl of very rotten fruit or vegetables

Every day, each of us makes choices about the way we want to do things. The Bible is there to help us with life-saving 'recipes' for living our lives with and for Jesus. Without a recipe for life, we are bound to end up lost and in a muddle.

Show the children the cookery book and ask them what it is and why we need recipes, helping them to grasp that a recipe means step-by-step instructions for making delicious food.

Ask them what their favourite food is and then tell them that you want to try out a really

wonderful stew (or something). Produce the revolting, rotting bits and pieces. Indulge in a bit of acting—for example, *'What's wrong with squidgy, black carrots? I'm sure once I've cooked them they'll be just as delicious as the ones in this picture…'*

Ask the children if they'd like to come to lunch with you today! The point is that to make yummy food, you need good, fresh ingredients. Every day we are like cooks as we choose and use ingredients for our lives.

Say that in the Bible there is a story about a man who lived his life according to a recipe where the main ingredients were greed and dishonesty. He lived at the time of Jesus and his name was Zacchaeus.

Ask the children what they know about Zacchaeus. It is far more effective to involve them in piecing together Zacchaeus' story than simply to read the account that follows. I have included the account, however, both in order to patch up any information gaps and because there may be children who have never heard of Zacchaeus before. If you feel your group will profit from hearing the whole Zacchaeus story, then either act it out yourself as you tell it, or get some of the more outgoing children to mime the roles of Zacchaeus, Jesus and the crowds as you narrate.

Zacchaeus was loathed by all around him because his job involved collecting money from his own people and giving it to the Romans who were in power at the time. Not only was he working for the conquerors who had taken over Israel, but he was also quietly helping himself to some of the money and becoming increasingly rich. Although his bank account was getting nice and big, Zacchaeus himself was rather small. That was why, one day, when Jesus was passing through his

town, Zacchaeus ran ahead of the pushing, shoving crowds and climbed up a tree. He was curious about this man, Jesus, who was making such a big stir and he wanted to be sure of a good view. From his leafy viewpoint he stared down as the man about whom he had heard so much slowly approached. Suddenly, without warning, Jesus stopped right underneath the tree and looked straight up into Zacchaeus' face. Then he spoke directly to the surprised little man in the tree.

'Zacchaeus! Come down at once! I must stay at your house today!'

This was mind-boggling, amazing, unbelievable! But even as Zacchaeus began the undignified process of climbing out of the tree, the crowds around him began voicing their disapproval.

'Why is Jesus choosing to be *his* guest, of all people?' they grumbled loudly. 'Everyone knows Zacchaeus is a dishonest rascal!'

Jesus knew this too. But he also knew that this made Zacchaeus the ideal candidate for receiving his help. He had come to seek and to save anyone who had followed a bad recipe for living their lives and was now lost and floundering, like Zacchaeus. And that's when Zacchaeus decided to follow a different recipe for his life. He reached the ground and spoke to Jesus.

'Look, Lord! I'm going to do things differently from now on. Here and now I give half of all that I have to the poor. And I'm going to pay back everyone I've cheated, four times the amount.'

That sounded like a completely different way of living, and Jesus knew that Zacchaeus meant what he said. Zacchaeus had been heading the wrong way. The recipe he had been using for his life was going to be a flop in the long run and had already made him a lot of enemies. But now Jesus had sought him out, saved him and given him a new recipe to follow—a recipe that involved following Jesus and putting right the things he had done wrong.

What kind of ingredients do the children think are important for their lives? What kind of recipe are they following? Here's an example of a recipe some children might follow:

1. Get up.
2. Grab the remains of the Frosties and leave your sister the cornflakes, which she doesn't like.
3. Get to the front of the bus queue by using your elbows.
4. Quickly copy your maths homework off a friend when you get to school.
5. A friend has brought some cakes to share. Decide which is the biggest and get it before anyone else can.

What would be a good name for that recipe? 'Me first'? 'Selfish Pie'? Gather suggestions.

We are all cooks, but Jesus is the master chef and we can always go to him for help as we struggle with our recipes! As he says of himself in Luke 19:10: *'The Son of Man came to look for and to save people who are lost.'*

A GAME AND AN EGGSPERIMENT

You need:
☆ A hard-boiled egg
☆ A glass bottle (not too narrow)
☆ A packet of matches
☆ Paper and pencil for each child
☆ Appropriate 'eggy' prizes

A hard-boiled egg is placed on top of a bottle. It looks impossible for the egg to fit inside the bottle. It seemed equally impossible for Jesus to lower himself and not only enter Zacchaeus' house as his guest, but also to enter his life and change it. But with a spark of faith, anything is possible! You should experiment with this first, before you do it with the children!

Give each child paper and pencil. Tell them that as the story was all about eggs, they are now going to see a rather 'eggy' experiment. Every time they hear the word 'egg', (which might be incorporated in a word in rather an unusual way), they should quickly draw a little egg on their paper. See who gets the right number of egg words. Use the following sentence to show them how 'egg' will be incorporated into words:

'For all those getting the right number of **egg** words, there will be an **eggstraordinary** prize!'

We heard in our story about **eggsploding eggs**. Here is a very **eggciting eggsperiment** to show the **eggstraordinary** way in which Jesus is prepared to enter the lives not only of characters like Zacchaeus, but also of people like you and me. Let me **eggsplain**.

Here we have a hard-boiled **egg**, and here we have an empty bottle. Imagine the **egg** says to the bottle, '**Eggscuse** me, may I make a little **eggscursion** and come in and visit you today?'

Do you remember Jesus surprising Zacchaeus with a similar **uneggspected** request?

Now, **eggsamine** this bottle carefully. Do you think the **egg** can fit inside it? It is no **eggsaggeration** to say that it would be an **eggceedingly** tight squeeze! The **eggsterior** of the **egg** is simply too **eggcessively** wide.

Jesus would also like to come into our lives. But how can that be? Jesus is almighty, powerful and perfect. How on earth can he come into the life of little old **eggocentric** you or me? I **eggspect** you can see that fitting Jesus into our lives would be even more **eggcessive** than fitting this **egg** in the bottle.

However, Jesus volunteered to do something **eggceptional** to make this impossible scenario possible. He allowed his body to be broken—he died on the cross. *(Break the shell of the egg, peel it and place it on the bottle.)*

Christians believe that lives without Jesus are **eggsactly** like this bottle—empty. The Bible tells us that Jesus has allowed his **eggsternal** shell—his body—to be broken so that he can be with us always, as part of our lives. But how can this be? Unless… *(light a match and hold it up)* unless there's a little spark (it only takes a tiny one)—a spark of faith which says: 'Yes, it may seem impossible. But if Jesus says he wants to be part of our lives, then maybe it isn't impossible after all.'

(Lift up the shelled egg, carefully drop a couple of freshly lit matches inside the bottle and quickly place the egg on top of it again. The matches burn up all the oxygen in the bottle and, as a result, the egg is sucked in.)

It's **eggstremely** simple. As simple as this little **eggsercise**. Christians believe that no one is **eggsempt**. We do not have to **eggcell** or be **eggcellent**. We are all in **eggsactly** the same position as Zacchaeus—little, imperfect people. But Christians believe that Jesus makes a difference to our lives. Look at the **eggshilarating** change in Zacchaeus, for **eggsample**. He **eggchanged** dishonesty for honest generosity.

Christians believe that anyone can ask Jesus into their life. We don't have to be **eggsperts** to do it. It's not **eggspensive**. It's an **eggsclusive** offer that's absolutely free! But it will make a difference to our whole **eggsistence**. It's **eggsquisite**!

(There are forty 'egg' words!)

TEASPOON PRAYER

Thanks: Thank you that in the Bible we can find helpful recipes for the big adventure of life.

Sorry: Sorry that we sometimes choose to follow the wrong recipes.

Please: Please help us to make the right choices.

SOMETHING TO MAKE

Your very own recipe book

You need:
* ☆ One ringbinder for each child
* ☆ Scraps of colourful wrapping paper or pictures of food from magazine recipes
* ☆ Glue
* ☆ Enough scissors for everybody
* ☆ Clear sticky-backed plastic

Each child can make his or her own personal recipe book.

The children can glue a collage of cut-out pictures on to the covers of their folders. They should make sure that their name and the title 'Recipes for life' are clearly displayed. When the glue is dry, each collage can be covered with the sticky-backed plastic to stop the pictures peeling off. Each week these recipe books can be brought out and the children can be given copies of the recipe, the song and the scripture reference to file away. They can also be encouraged to write their own teaspoon prayers.

Chapter 2

THE LITTLE BLUE STONE AND THE GBB

'I am the way, the truth, and the life!' Jesus answered. 'Without me, no one can go to the Father.'

JOHN 14:6

Have you ever thought about how each time you wake up in the morning, your feet take you in a certain direction? Maybe they first take you to the bathroom, then down to breakfast, then off to school… Just think how many steps we take, each day, each week, each month, each year. But our feet don't decide where to go on their own. Our brains make the decisions that tell our feet where to go, our hands what to do, our mouths what to say, our minds what to think. There are all sorts of different ways we can choose to lead our lives. Let's hear what happened to Andy when his teacher gave him a little blue stone and told him it could influence his life.

One day, Andy came home from school with a present from his teacher. All the children who had filled up their reading cards had been given one. It was a little polished blue stone on a chain.

'Miss Barnes says that it has special energy and if I wear it all the time, it will give me good luck,' said Andy. Proudly, he hung it round his neck.

'It's very pretty,' said Anna enviously. 'Can I try it on?'

They were all out in the garden, where Mum

was collecting slugs out of the vegetable patch. She left them in a bucket and came over to have a look.

'Can I see?' said Mum and she took the smooth, cool stone into her hand. She held it up to the light and let it shimmer in the evening sunshine. 'It's beautiful,' she said. 'But you know, Andy, I would disagree with your teacher that it holds any powers.'

'Don't you want me to wear it, then?' asked Andy.

Mum looked down at his disappointed face.

'You can wear it if you want,' she said, 'but wear it for what it is—a reward for finishing your reading card.' And she went back to the slugs, some of which were trying to escape by sliming their way up the sides of the bucket.

The next day, Andy came down to breakfast with the stone hanging round his neck.

'You're not going to wear it to school, are you?' asked Mum sleepily as she took her first life-giving sip of coffee.

'Oh Mum, it's OK,' said Andy. 'After all, Miss Barnes said the stone's energy would do us good.'

'Do you really believe that?'

'Well, I have to believe quite a few things she says,' said Andy defensively. 'Like, for example, that the world is round, or that a spider has six legs.'

'Eight!' shouted Robby triumphantly.

'But those are things that you can look up in books or test for yourself by catching a spider,' said Mum.

'And this stone is something I can test, too,' said Andy. 'That's why I want to wear it today. I could do with a bit of good luck—we've got a maths test.'

The first thing that happened on the way to school was that Andy had to run back because he had forgotten his swimming stuff. On his way to the bus stop again, he spotted a spider in the hedge and caught it. Not only did he discover that it really did have eight legs, but he also missed the school bus. He stood panting at the bus stop, watching the bus disappear round the corner, and was just wondering what to do when a car drew up.

'Jump in, it's your lucky day!' said a familiar voice and Andy recognized Jim.

'Wow, Jim, thanks,' said Andy, scrambling in. 'And thanks to this, too,' he added, holding up his blue stone. 'This stone has special energy. I think it made you come along when I missed the bus.'

Jim glanced sideways at the stone as he drove.

'Who's been putting nonsense like that in your young head, then?' he asked, grinning.

'Well, I'm testing it out today,' explained Andy. 'My teacher said it would bring me luck. I'm going to wear it and see if it really does.'

'I don't believe in all that rubbish,' said Jim, 'but there's plenty of people who do.'

He suddenly swerved off the main road into a tree-lined layby where several large lorries were parked.

'How much time have you got before school starts?' he asked. Andy looked at his watch.

'About three quarters of an hour,' he said.

Jim slapped his knee.

'That'll do!' he said. 'I want to invite you to the best breakfast you ever had in your whole life', and he pointed at a large, white trailer on which was painted in bright red letters: 'Jim's caff: All-day breakfast; hamburgers; hotdogs; chips; beverages, etc.'

'Is that yours?' asked Andy.

'It is,' said Jim, proudly.

'But I've already had breakfast,' said Andy, wishing he hadn't.

'Oh, come on—a growing lad like you!' said Jim. 'I'm sure you could fit in a bit more.' And Andy decided he could.

Inside the trailer, there was the delicious smell of frying bacon mingled with the rather less appetizing odour of cigarette smoke. Several men were sitting in a smoky haze on high stools at a counter, some reading the paper, some chatting, but all busy with plates heaped full of food.

'Morning, Mabel!' called Jim to the lady behind the counter. 'Two GBBs please and we'll take them outside. Ta, love.' And he led Andy behind the trailer, where there was a striped awning stretched over several tables and chairs. Jim pulled a chair out for Andy.

'Thanks,' said Andy. 'What's a GBB, Jim?'

'A Great Big British, of course,' he answered, flicking a few crumbs off the table.

'British what?'

'British breakfast—and you won't get better anywhere,' he said proudly.

As he spoke, Mabel came out bearing two plates piled high with fried eggs, still-sizzling bacon, beans, tomatoes, mushrooms, fried bread and sausages.

'Wow!' said Andy, and Jim beamed.

'Now, before you get tucked into that, we'll just give your mum a quick buzz so she knows where you are,' said Jim, getting out his mobile and tapping Andy's number in. He boomed a quick explanation and then, in exactly the same cheery voice as he'd used for the phone, with his smily eyes wide open and dancing, Jim said: 'Thanks, Lord for this great grub, and thanks that you're with us two for breakfast. Amen. Tuck in!'

And he and Andy both picked up their knives and forks and attacked their plates. The food was delicious. Andy always loved a cooked breakfast (a rare treat in his family) but somehow it tasted even better than usual, under the striped canvas, with Jim guzzling away on the other side of the table. Andy speared one of his eggs with his knife and scooped up the glistening yellow yolk on to his fried bread. Jim watched him in delight.

'I can see that's going down the right way,' he said approvingly. 'But watch that stone you've got dangling round your neck. It's getting a face-lift!' For as Andy had bent over his plate, the stone hanging round his neck had taken a dip in a mixture of egg yolk and tomato sauce. Andy licked it off.

'Now, about that stone there,' continued Jim, thoughtfully. 'When I was about your age, I had a bracelet. I wore it all the time, because I thought it brought me luck. I got in with the wrong crowd and I got to taking things from the shops. It started off small—a can of beans here, a Mars bar there—but it got bigger. I always wore

my bracelet when I went shoplifting because I thought it kept me safe, and I went for years without getting caught. But one day, when I was involved in a big job, I got caught by the police, and I was in trouble. Deep trouble.'

Andy stared. Jim shoplifting? He could hardly believe it.

'Well,' said Jim, attacking his bacon afresh, 'the police let me off with a fine and a warning and I decided to try to do my best not to steal any more. I left the police station, but I was scared. I didn't know what to do. I didn't know where to go. Then suddenly this policeman came running after me. I tell you, I very nearly took off. I thought they were after me again. But all he wanted was to give me back my bracelet.

'"You forgot this," he said, handing it to me. Then he looked me straight in the eye and he said something that really surprised me. He said, "If you want to make a new start, I'll give you a tip. Make your new start with God. He'll help you." I didn't know what to say. I just looked at him. Then I said, "I don't know the way."

'"Jesus does though," he said. Then he pointed behind me. I hadn't realized, but I was standing just in front of a church and up on the wall there was this huge poster. It said in great big coloured letters, "Jesus says, 'I am the way, the truth and the life.'"'

Andy squashed the last few beans on to his fork and listened, fascinated. 'But what does that mean?' he asked.

'I didn't really understand at that moment either,' said Jim. 'But that copper became a friend of mine. He showed me that it meant Jesus is all we need. No bracelets, no stolen goods, nothing apart from trust in Jesus. Cling on to him and he carries us in the right direction.' Jim paused and wiped his mouth. 'When I understood that,' he said, 'I made a new start in life. And with God's help, everything has turned out quite differently to what it looked like all those years ago. But we'd better get you to school now. We'll just make it if the traffic behaves itself.'

Feeling pleasantly full, Andy followed him to the car and soon they arrived in front of the school gates.

'Don't forget!' said Jim as Andy got out. 'Jesus is the way, the truth, and the life.'

Andy shrugged. It was all a bit hard to understand.

'But I've had pretty good luck so far,' he thought to himself as he waved goodbye. 'I'm going to go on seeing if this stone does make my day better.' And he ran into school.

That afternoon, Andy just couldn't wait to get home. He ran up the garden path and burst into the house. 'Mum!' he shouted. 'Mum, where are you?'

'I'm out here,' came a distant voice from the garden. Andy dashed through the back door.

'This is what I think of Miss Barnes' stone,' he said, pulling it out of his pocket and dropping it into the bucket of slugs. Mum looked up at him from where she was kneeling, utterly astonished.

'Whatever happened?' she asked.

'Well, first of all, I had this long chat with Jim and that was really interesting, but I thought I'd still go on testing if the stone brought me luck. The maths test was awful—the stone was no help there. Then we had swimming and my friend Barry did this really fantastic dive from the highest board. He was still wearing his lucky stone round his neck and it kind of bounced up and knocked out his front tooth!'

For once, Mum was speechless.

Pikelets

(Breakfast pancakes)

These little pancakes are also a great way of making a special breakfast. Eat them with butter and jam or maple syrup. They can be made in advance and eaten cold, or hot, straight out of the pan.

☆ 2 cups self-raising flour
☆ 1/2 teaspoon bicarbonate of soda
☆ 1 cup milk
☆ 4 teaspoons sugar
☆ Pinch of salt
☆ 2 eggs
☆ 50g melted butter

1. Combine all dry ingredients together and then gradually add eggs and milk, mixing all the time.

2. Heat a non-stick frying pan or griddle with a little oil or butter.

3. Drop tablespoonfuls of the mixture into the pan.

4. Allow to spread out and cook, then turn with a spatula and cook the other side.

LIFE IS LIKE A JOURNEY

I wonder if you have ever thought of life as a journey? From the moment we're born, we start off on the journey of life. One of the first things we do on this journey is to fill our nappy. We get good at doing this very quickly. Then comes our first smile, and our mums and dads, grannies and grandpas and all our aunts, uncles, friends and relations melt away and think we're the most adorable and wonderful baby in the world. Then we learn to hold up our head, which is a bit wobbly at first, and then we learn to sit up. And all the time we are developing new and very important skills which we will need for the rest of life's journey, like saying 'ga goo', or 'mama' and even eventually, after a few years, 'two plus two is four'.

Often things happen on this journey that we are not prepared for—happy things and sad things. Can you think of any such things?

People have different ways of coping with the journey of life. Some people think that *money* is a very helpful friend for the journey of life, and they spend a lot of time trying to get as much as possible.

Lots of people think *possessions* are very important for the journey of life—nice cars, trendy clothes, and the latest technology.

A surprising number of people place their trust in *horoscopes* or the energy of stones or things like *feng shui* as a help for living their lives. God tells us in the Bible that a fascination with the supernatural is dangerous.

Sadly, some people think *smoking, alcohol* or *drugs* are necessary for life's journey, but in the end those things only make the journey harder.

Where does the journey of life end up? Where are we all heading?

The answer is very simple and it is the same for everyone, whether we are millionaires with swimming pools, saunas and huge houses or whether we just live in a tiny hut. We are all going to end up the same one day—dead!

But Christians believe that that is not the end of the journey. The Bible says that after death there is life with God. Christians believe that the only way of finding the right direction for the journey of life is by placing their trust in Jesus and allowing him to guide them along the right path.

A GAME TO PLAY

The journey of life

You need:
☆ An obstacle course to help illustrate the concept of life as a journey. As children are going to navigate it blindfolded, make sure you set it up using soft objects (cushions, bean-bags, hoops, sheets of newspaper held up by other children, balloons and so on).
☆ A crown—the goal to be reached at the end of the obstacle course.

The obstacle course represents the journey of life and the goal is to navigate it and reach the crown at the other end, blindfolded.

Ask for a volunteer (choose a confident child) and bind her eyes with a scarf. Tell all the other children that they have to be absolutely silent. Explain to the volunteer that she is blindfolded to represent the fact that we cannot see into the future: we don't know all that is going to happen in our lives. For this reason too, as soon as the volunteer starts navigating the course, two or three of the watching children should very quietly change the position of some of the things. By holding up a hoop to climb through, waving silk

scarves, throwing balloons around, or holding a sheet of newspaper in front of the blindfolded child, they should make it harder for the child to reach the goal. Stop the child after a short time and take the blindfold off. Show her how everything has changed and how far away she was from achieving the goal.

Then ask for another volunteer, blindfold him and explain that this time, the other children can shout helpful things to guide him. Encourage the children to shout so loudly that the volunteer won't be able to understand what anyone is saying. Again move all the things around as soon as he is blindfolded.

Ask for a third volunteer and blindfold her. Tell the other children to change things on the obstacle course as before, and to guide her by shouting. But this time, take the third volunteer yourself by the hand and lead her through the course, using quiet verbal guidance where necessary, so that she is led straight to the crown. Ask the children who made it to the crown.

Yes, the third child got there! Although blindfolded like the other two, this child wasn't alone, like person A. Also, she wasn't distracted by all the things in the world clamouring for attention, like person B. The third volunteer was being helped by someone who could see the way forward, someone who was holding on, guiding and helping her. In real life, Christians believe that Jesus is our guide. That's what Jim meant in our story. In the Bible, Jesus tells us that he is the way and the truth and the life. In the same way that the third volunteer was led through the obstacle course, Christians believe that we can trust Jesus to lead us through life.

A SONG TO SING

*In the tummy of their mummy once
two babies lay
And they chatted as they practised
shooting goals all day.
They discussed the latest gossip
and collapsed in mirth
At the rumour going round about
life after birth.*

Li-li-li-li-life!
Li-li-li-li-life!
Li-li-li-li-li-li-life!
We're grateful for the gift of life.

It is funny; earning money really takes all day.
After birth those babes grew up and now they
get good pay.
They don't have much time for chatting
but collapse in mirth
At the rumour going round about
life after death.

Li-li-li-li-life!
Li-li-li-li-life!
Li-li-li-li-li-li-life!
We're grateful for the gift of,
grateful for the gift of...

(The chorus is sung again, at the same time as the third verse is sung.)

What a mystery throughout history
is the empty grave.
Jesus died in pain but rose again,
new life he gave.
If we wish him to, he'll lead us through
our trials and strife,
For Jesus is the way, the truth and life!

TEASPOON PRAYER

Thanks: Thank you, Jesus, that with you we are never alone. Thank you that you can guard us and guide us on the journey of life.

Sorry: Sorry that we sometimes forget about you and try to do things on our own.

Please: Please help us to be able to sort out the true things that we need for life from the unimportant or even dangerous things.

Life

In the tummy of their mummy once two babies lay
And they chatted as they practised shooting goals all day.
They discussed the latest gossip and collapsed in mirth
At the rumour going round about life after birth.

Li-li-li-li-li-life!
Li-li-li-li-li-life!
Li-li-li-li-li-li-li-life!
We're grateful for the gift of life.

It is funny; earning money really takes all day.
After birth those babes grew up and now they get good pay.
They don't have much time for chatting but collapse in mirth
At the rumour going round about life after death.

Li-li-li-li-li-life!
Li-li-li-li-li-life!
Li-li-li-li-li-li-li-life!
We're grateful for the gift of, grateful for the gift of...

(The chorus is sung again, at the same time as the third verse is sung.)

What a mystery throughout history is the empty grave.
Jesus died in pain but rose again, new life he gave.
If we wish him to, he'll lead us through our trials and strife,
For Jesus is the way, the truth and life!

Reproduced with permission from *Does Jesus Like Cake?* published by BRF 2003 (1 84101 319 6)

Chapter 3

THE LOGS, THE SPECKS AND MRS BO

Don't condemn others, and God won't condemn you. God will be as hard on you as you are on others! He will treat you exactly as you treat them.

You can see the speck in your friend's eye, but you don't notice the log in your own eye. How can you say, 'My friend, let me take the speck out of your eye,' when you don't see the log in your own eye? You're nothing but show-offs! First, take the log out of your own eye. Then you can see how to take the speck out of your friend's eye.

MATTHEW 7:1–5

The next day was a Saturday and as Robby and Anna had both been very jealous to hear about Andy's treat with Jim, Andy went into his parents' bedroom early in the morning, to ask Mum if he could cook a GBB for the whole family. She was half asleep at the time, and so, for the sake of peace, said 'yes'.

Any further peace was out of the question, however, as every five minutes, Andy came charging into their room to ask questions about how much fat, which ring to use, where the frying pan was and if she had any sausages.

In the end Mum got up, just in time to stop the bacon going up in flames. However, when everything was ready, Andy insisted that she went back to bed and he and the others then served their parents a full, if slightly blackened, English breakfast on a tray in their bedroom.

Perhaps this was why everyone was still in their pyjamas when Mrs Bloomsbury-Oliver arrived with her teenage daughter Zara for Zara's piano lesson, which Mum had totally forgotten about.

Mrs Bloomsbury-Oliver (or Mrs BO, as Dad called her in private) was not well-liked by the three children. They couldn't really define why.

Anna went to answer the doorbell, and when she saw who it was she shouted in her sweetest tones, 'Mum! Get out of bed! Mrs BO's here for Zara's lesson.'

Dad groaned and Mum leapt as though she'd been stung by a wasp, scattering bits of bacon rind everywhere. Two minutes later, slightly crumpled but fully dressed, she emerged from her room.

'Oh, that's quite all right, Sue, I'm sure you deserve a lie-in,' boomed Mrs BO in response to Mum's apologies. 'But do you think we could open a few windows? The smell of bacon is delicious but a little over-powering when it gets burnt, wouldn't you agree?'

Mum fluttered around opening windows and, as she did so, told Mrs BO about how Andy had made the breakfast, inspired by his visit to Jim's caff.

'You don't mean that lorry drivers' café just off the roundabout at Dorly, do you?' asked Mrs BO in horror.

'That's right!' joined in Andy, excitedly. 'You should go there for breakfast, Mrs Bloomsbury-Oliver. I had the best breakfast I've ever had in my whole life!'

Mrs BO looked at him for a second, then turned to Mum and said in a low voice, 'I'm surprised you let him go there, Sue. I'm not sure how hygienic it is. He might catch something. And believe me, there are some rough characters who go there. As for the proprietor—James Newton, I believe his name is—well, I know for a fact that he was in terrible trouble with the police, oh, years ago when George was just finishing his training.'

Mum's lips set themselves in a thin line.

'I know Jim Newton well,' she said firmly. 'He goes to our church.'

'Really?' said Mrs BO, surprised. 'I've never seen him there.'

'That's because he does the Sunday school most mornings,' said Mum. 'He's a great Sunday school teacher and, as it happens, a very dear friend. In fact, at the moment he's living downstairs.'

'Oh, I didn't know,' said Mrs BO, looking slightly uncomfortable. She hastily endeavoured to change the subject. 'Now George and I love to go to Barnstables for breakfast,' she said brightly. 'Have you ever tried it?' Barnstables was a new restaurant that had just opened in a converted barn in the village. Mum said she wasn't in the habit of going out to breakfast, she preferred it served in bed.

'Well, it's also *the* place to go for dinner,' continued Mrs BO enthusiastically. 'The food is exquisite. They have a French chef—André—a most charming young man, and so talented. He gave me the recipe for his crème brulée. Now, Zara, get your music out. I'll be with you again in an hour.'

Zara, who was tall and spotty, obediently got out her music and very soon the children could hear her picking her awkward way through *Für Elise*.

At lunchtime, the children started talking about Mrs Bloomsbury-Oliver.

'What a mean old bag to talk about Jim like that,' said Andy indignantly. 'It's true, Mum, Jim was once in trouble with the police. He told me about it yesterday. But he's different now. He follows Jesus. And I bet Mrs BO doesn't, even though she sits in church every Sunday.'

'And have you heard her sing?' chimed in Robby. He got up from his chair, pulled the cushion out from beneath him and stuffed it up his jumper. Then he straddled his legs, sticking out his chest, and, with a great deal of vibrato, began to warble in a high voice to the tune of 'Hark the herald angels sing':

> 'Hark! the herald angel thinks
> Mrs BO really stinks.
> Peace on earth and mercy mild,
> So does her revolting child.'

He sat down again, looking quite stunned at his own creative genius, while the rest of the family giggled helplessly. His imitation had been very life-like.

'Stop it, stop it,' gasped Mum, but it was too late. Dad had that special expression on his face reserved for his poetic moments. He was obviously getting a little over-excited. He continued with the same tune:

> 'Sadly Mr BO sighs,
> "Yes, I know she's oversize,
> But at Barnstables the food
> Is so very, very good..."
> Hark! The hungry gourmet sings,
> Barnstables is fit for kings.'

'All right! That's quite enough,' said Mum. 'Stop it. Now this is all very funny, but do you realize that we're all doing exactly the same as Mrs BO did this morning? And by the way, Anna, please use her full name when she is listening.'

'What d'you mean, Mum?' asked Robby.

'Well, you're all looking for specks and ignoring logs,' said Mum. 'Just like she did.'

She looked at the circle of blank faces around her (apart from Dad's, who was obviously still far away in the realms of poetry) and continued, 'It's very easy to see when other people get it wrong, isn't it? If only we were so good at noticing and correcting our own bad behaviour.'

'Yes, but what was it you said before?' asked Robby. 'Something about lecks and splogs?'

'Specks and logs,' corrected Mum. 'Jesus said that noticing the things other people do wrong is like noticing tiny specks of sawdust in everybody else's eyes, but not realizing that your own are so blocked up with a great big chunky log that you can hardly see straight yourself.'

Anxiously, Anna looked deep into her mother's

eyes. Then she jumped up from the table and ran into the bathroom. They heard her clambering up on to the bathroom chair to gaze at her face in the mirror. She ran back looking relieved.

'No wood anywhere,' she reported.

Mum laughed.

'Jesus didn't mean real wood, Anna. It was just a way of drawing a picture with words. But it really is easier to get all het up about faults in other people and yet quite happily ignore your own. I know I do it all the time.'

'Hear, hear!' said Dad, coming out of his reverie suddenly.

'But Mrs BO was wrong to say that about Jim,' objected Andy.

'Yes, maybe she was,' agreed Mum. 'But at the same time, we're wrong to judge her, too. We have to remember that all of us make mistakes.'

At that moment the phone rang and Mum went to answer it. She was away for a long time. When she came back, the kitchen was empty— apart from piles of dirty crockery beside the sink, well-licked pudding spoons scattered on the table, a large number of squashed green peas on the floor, a lone potato underneath a chair and Dad behind the newspaper. Mum put her hands on her hips and roared, 'Hey, you lot, I've got a surprise for you! But before I tell you, I want this mess cleared up!'

Reluctantly, the children slunk back into the kitchen.

'It's easy to complain about how awful Mrs BO is and then scoff your food and sneak away, leaving me to clear everything up,' she said with a grin. Then she continued, 'You'll never guess who that was on the phone.'

'Who?' everybody chorused.

'Mrs BO,' answered Mum. 'She rang up to apologize for what she said about Jim and to invite us all out tomorrow for brunch at Barnstables, after church.'

Mum smiled at their astonished expressions.

'But I don't think I want to go,' said Andy slowly. 'Not after what she said about Jim.'

'Don't you worry about that,' said Mum. 'I'm going to make sure I introduce her to Jim and she's going to get on with him like a house on fire. She likes his restaurant, after all.'

'What?' said Andy. 'She said…'

'She said that at Barnstables the food is exquisite,' said Mum, smugly.

'Yes, but…'

'And I happen to know that Barnstables is Jim's newest venture. His trailers have done so well that, after much prayer, he bought that barn, had it done up and made it into a restaurant. That French cook André used to be in prison for shoplifting. He was trained to cook by Jim himself.'

Mars bar logs

(Naughty but nice—no baking required)

★ 6 Mars bars
★ 150g butter or margarine
★ 2 tablespoons golden syrup
★ 200g Rice Krispies
★ 200g chocolate cake covering

1. Get the children to chop up the Mars bars into small pieces. Melt together with the butter and syrup in the microwave or over a bowl of hot water.

2. When mixed and melted, add the Rice Krispies and mix thoroughly so that all the Rice Krispies are covered.

3. Press mixture into a lightly greased baking tin.

4. Melt the chocolate cake covering (either in microwave or over water) and spread over the Krispie mixture.

5. Place in fridge to harden, then cut into logs and serve.

As you make the logs, you can talk about how little specks (like the Krispies) add up to make logs. Logs need to be got rid of. These ones are easy to dispose of— just eat them!

Reproduced with permission from *Does Jesus Like Cake?* published by BRF 2003 (1 84101 319 6)

NOBODY IS PERFECT

'I could hardly believe my eyes!' Have you ever read that in a story or heard somebody say it? It's actually quite a wise thing to say. Often we believe what we think we see far too quickly and end up jumping to the wrong conclusions. In the story we've just heard, all sorts of people were firmly making up their minds about other people. Were they always right? And although, in films, mostly the 'baddies' stay bad and the 'goodies' stay good, that's not the case in real life. All of us have got the potential to do good or harm, and all of us need to forgive and be forgiven.

Jesus probably knew all too well how it felt to get a speck of sawdust in his eye, because his dad, Joseph, was a carpenter, and when carpenters are at work, then sawdust is flying all over the place. Maybe Jesus sometimes had to help his dad get things out of his eye.

Have you ever had anything in your eye? How does it feel? Have you ever helped someone to get something out of their eye? It's no good trying to help if one of your own eyes is all red and weepy and watery because there's something stuck in it. You just can't see properly if you have something in your own eye. Jesus made this very clear with his word-picture. The thought of telling someone that they really ought to get the speck of dust out of their eye when all the time the speaker doesn't even notice the huge log blocking his own vision is actually very funny! What Jesus is really saying with this first-century joke is that *nobody is perfect*! We all make mistakes, so we shouldn't get all cross about other people without taking a good, careful look at ourselves first.

We all know that Old Macdonald had a farm, don't we? But I wonder what he was actually like? And what about his wife? Although we know all about their pigs with an oink-oink here, and their cows with a moo-moo there, we don't know much about Old Mr and Mrs MacDonald. Well, here's a song that will help us to get to know them better.

A SONG TO SING

(To the tune of 'Old McDonald had a farm')

Verse one

Old McDonald liked to take
e-i-e-i-o
The very largest slice of cake.
e-i-e-i-o
With a cream slice here
And a cup cake there,
Here a scone, now it's gone,
Everywhere the plate is bare.
Old McDonald liked his cake,
e-i-e-i-o.

Leader pauses to ask these questions:

- Do you think it's OK to take the biggest, nicest slice of cake for yourself?
- What do you think Old McDonald looks like? Do you imagine him to be fat or thin?

- How do you think his wife feels about her husband's love of cake?

Leader says: Let's sing that again (you can join in the 'e-i-e-i-o's). Then I'll sing the next verse and you can see what Mrs McDonald feels.

(Sing verse one and then the following.)

Verse two

Old McDonald's wife said, 'Dave!'
e-i-e-i-o
'That's not the way you should behave!'
e-i-e-i-o
'When you're out with me
Eating cakes for tea,
Don't be rude, grabbing food,
Swallowing it down half chewed.'
Old McDonald's wife said, 'Dave!'
e-i-e-i-o.

Leader pauses to ask these questions:

- Do you feel sorry for Mrs McDonald?
- What do you think she looks like—fat or thin?

Leader says: We'll sing those two verses again, then listen carefully to see what Old McDonald has to say for himself when he answers his wife.

(Sing verse 1 and 2 and then the following.)

Verse three

Old McDonald went quite red.
e-i-e-i-o
'Look who's talking now,' he said.
e-i-e-i-o
'With a chomp-chomp here,
And a gulp-gulp there,
Here a bun, now there's none,

Everything lands in YOUR tum!'
Old McDonald went quite red.
e-i-e-i-o.

Leader pauses to ask these questions:

- Was Mrs McDonald cross with her husband just because it is impolite to eat so greedily, or was she just as bad herself?

Leader says: Let's start the song again at the beginning and see what happens next!

(Sing verses 1, 2 and 3 and then the following.)

Verse four

Now the purpose of this song
e-i-e-i-o
Is to show that both were wrong.
e-i-e-i-o
So before you judge
And then bear a grudge,
Have a check—log or speck
In your e-eye-e-eye-oh?
Make sure you aren't guilty too!
e-i-e-i-oh!

TEASPOON PRAYER

Thanks: Thank you, Lord Jesus, that you love us in spite of our specks and logs!

Sorry: Sorry that we find it so easy to criticize other people.

Please: Please help us to remember that you love us in spite of our faults. Help us to love and accept others even when we notice their faults.

Chapter 4

THE DUSTBIN

> *I pray to you, Lord! Please listen. Don't hide from me in my time of trouble. Pay attention to my prayer and quickly give an answer.*
>
> PSALM 102:1–2

The book of Psalms comes in the Old Testament (the first part of the Bible) and it contains lots of different prayers and songs. This psalm is the prayer of someone in great trouble. Just because we read the Bible and maybe try to find out the best 'recipes' for life, it doesn't mean we will never have problems or difficulties. Sometimes it might even feel as though God hasn't heard our prayers. Perhaps you have sometimes felt that God is not looking after you? You can tell God how you're feeling, like Robby does in the next story.

'We've got this new girl in our class,' said Robby one day as Mum was driving him to the hairdresser's. She had, after a long battle, persuaded him to come and get his hair cut. 'Her name is Jasmin Softic and she is *huge*—really, really fat.'

'Poor thing,' said Mum. 'How long has she been in your class?'

Robby considered. 'A few weeks,' he said.

'And has she found some friends?'

'She's found lots of enemies,' said Robby grimly. 'One of the boys in our class nicknamed her Jasmin the Dustbin and that's what they all call her now. Nobody will play with her.'

'Do you play with her?'

Robby looked scandalized.

'Oh, Mum, you just don't understand,' he said, heaving a sigh at her ignorance. 'I mean, not only is she the Dustbin, but she's also a Girl. That makes it even worse. If I'm nice to her, they'll laugh at me, too. But I really feel sorry for her. If she tries to join in anywhere, the others just tease her. Once, Jenny Mayhew had this lovely cake and she dropped it in a puddle by mistake. And Kevin Porter—he's the biggest boy in our class—said, "Put it in the Dustbin", and pointed at Jasmin. So Jenny went over to Jasmin and asked if she wanted the cake. And Jasmin, who hadn't seen it fall, was really pleased and she actually took a bite. Then all the girls screamed and said she'd probably got germs now. And now none of them will go near her in case they get her germs.'

'That sounds terrible,' said Mum. 'Wouldn't you hate that if it were you?'

'I hate it for her, too,' said Robby, helplessly. 'But I don't know what I can do.'

*

At 'Clip', an overpowering dose of hairdresser smell wafted out of the open door to greet them.

'Would you like to come over here and have a seat, love?' called the hairdresser, and Robby picked his way through the tufts of hair strewn all over the floor. He sat down and gazed at his face in the mirror while the hairdresser fiddled with his chair, getting it the right height.

'How would you like it?' she asked.

'Just a tiny bit shorter—so that it hardly looks any different,' he said hopefully.

'But so we don't have to come again too soon,' said Mum firmly.

Robby sighed, took one last look in the mirror, thought 'Goodbye, hair', and then closed his eyes and sat quite still while the scissors snipped noisily.

'Quiet little boy, isn't he?' said the hairdresser to Mum as she fussed around. How could she know that, inside his head, Robby was being far from quiet? He was praying—talking away to God, his heavenly father.

'Dear Lord,' he prayed. 'You can see how I'm feeling scared just now about what they'll say to me tomorrow about my hair at school. You know Jasmin in my class? She must feel like this every day, only worse. Please can you help her? And please help me to be a bit braver and to stick up for Jasmin when the others are mean to her. I bet you've got some recipe about that in your book, the Bible. And please help the others not to laugh at my new haircut tomorrow. Amen.'

*

The next morning, Robby slunk into the classroom as unobtrusively as possible, but Kevin Porter burst into loud guffaws when he saw him. 'Look! Robby's been run over by a lawnmower!' Luckily, however, he was just in the middle of bargaining for football stickers, and so nothing more was said.

Usually their teacher, Miss Jones, came to take the register before assembly, but this morning the bell rang and she still had not come. At first the children sat at their desks waiting expectantly, but gradually the noise level rose, and very soon Kevin Porter and his cronies were pelting everyone else with balls of screwed-up paper.

'Hey, come on, everyone!' roared Kevin suddenly. 'We don't want to be litterbugs! Let's clear up this lot *into the dustbin*!' And he managed to get the whole class aiming not just

paper balls, but also pencils, rubbers, shoes—anything they could lay their hands on—at Jasmin. She buried her head in her arms on the desk to shield herself from the onslaught. Suddenly, something snapped inside Robby and he jumped to his feet.

'I'm going to get a teacher!' he shouted above the racket and made for the door. Instantly, Kevin and Clive jumped to their feet and hurled themselves on him.

'Guard the door, Tolhurst!' Kevin ordered one of his group. 'So Sissy here wants to get a teacher, does he?' he jeered. 'Just when we're having so much fun.'

Robby struggled and broke free. He ran towards the door, but someone stretched out their foot and tripped him up. He fell heavily and hit his elbow against a desk.

'Stay there!' yelled Kevin. Robby sprang up and began to push his way through the children thronging round the door, but there were too many against him. Down he went again and he felt a surge of panic as thumps rained down on him. Many hands were grappling with his shirt and trousers, he felt someone stuff something up his jumper, and a foot kicked him in the stomach.

But then, quite suddenly, the babble of voices stopped and there was a deathly hush. Robby stood up, his head reeling, and caught the full force of the deputy head's steely glare as she walked into the classroom.

'Sit down, all of you, at once, in your places,' she commanded. 'Now, I do not want any shouting out. If you want to answer my question, please raise your hand. Where is Miss Jones?'

Kevin Porter's hand shot up.

'Yes?'

'Miss Jones hasn't come yet. Me and Clive here have been trying to fetch a teacher, but that boy there wouldn't let us,' and he pointed at Robby.

Robby leapt up. 'That's not true!' he shouted.

'I said no shouting out,' said Mrs Hales icily, but at that moment there was a knock and Mr Roberts, the headmaster, poked his head round the door.

'Ah, Mrs Hales. So glad to find you here. Could I just have a quick word outside?' he said.

Mrs Hales glared at the class.

'I want silence,' she said and swept out, leaving the door ajar.

Kevin Porter spoke in a loud whisper:

'If any of you tells,' he said, 'me and Clive and Tolly will bash you up. If you stick to my story, only *he* will get into trouble,' and he pointed at Robby. 'Otherwise you'll all be in trouble, not only with me, but with Hales. And nobody's got no proof,' he added as an afterthought.

'That's where you're wrong,' said a voice that trembled a little, and Jasmin stood up. 'I saw Andrew Tolhurst, Kevin Porter and Clive Leatherson all take their chewing gum out of their mouths and make a great big ball out of it and stuff it up Robby's jumper,' she said. 'I can use that as evidence.'

So that was what that uncomfortable lump was. Robby twisted himself round and investigated. Oh, yuk! His shirt, trousers and jumper were all stuck together with a gluey, sticky, revolting mass of soggy gum. He felt sick. And he wondered what Mum would say.

'Great evidence,' sneered Kevin. 'Anyone could have done that. No one can prove that was us.'

'Oh yes they can,' said Jasmin. 'My Dad is a forensic scientist. He works for the police. He can easily test whose spit is in the gum. He does that kind of thing all the time.'

'But we won't be needing his services, thank you, dear,' said Mrs Hales sweetly, as she entered the classroom again. 'We teachers are neither so deaf nor so stupid as most children seem to think. Stand up... er... it's Robby, isn't it?'

'Yes,' said Robby, standing up. His knees were trembling.

'Turn around. Let me see the gum.'

Robby obeyed.

'Right. We'll ring your mother and ask if she can bring you some fresh clothes. And as for you three boys at the back, you are to go straight to Mr Roberts, who is waiting for you in his study. It won't surprise me if you have to pay for some new clothes for Robby. Chewing gum is impossible to remove.'

Kevin, Clive and Andrew Tolhurst got to their feet.

'But miss, it weren't just us,' objected Kevin as they got to the door.

'Go!' said Mrs Hales, very softly.

They went.

'Get out your English books, children, and turn to page 34,' said Mrs Hales calmly, getting out her mobile phone. 'What's your phone number, dear?' she said to Robby.

That afternoon, when school was over, Robby ran after Jasmin as she made her way through the playground.

'D'you want to come and play at my house tomorrow?' he panted.

She smiled at him—and what a smile! Her whole face suddenly lit up and shone as though someone had switched on a light inside. For a second, Robby almost felt as though he could stretch out and warm himself in the joy that smile radiated.

'That would be great!' she said. 'I'll ask my mum.'

'Jasmin,' said Robby, 'is your dad really a forensic scientist?' Her smile faded. Then she said simply, 'I don't even have a dad', and she turned and walked towards the school gates.

Robby stared after her. That night in bed he prayed, 'Please help Jasmin to find out she has a heavenly father, too.'

Jammy smilies

Make these delicious 'smilies' for someone and watch their face light up with a smile too!

* 400g flour
* 200g butter
* 3 egg yolks
* 100g sugar
* 50g ground hazelnuts (can be omitted and replaced by 50g extra flour and 1 teaspoon cinnamon in the case of nut allergy)
* 1/2 cup strawberry jam mixed with the juice of a lemon
* 1/2 cup powdered sugar for dusting over at the end.

That evening, Robby told Jim the whole story, even about the way Jasmin smiled when he asked her to play. That was why, when she did come the next day, Jim invited her and Robby down to his kitchen and taught them how to bake 'jammy smilies', the happiest biscuits in the world.

If you are making these with a group of children, it's easier to take the dough ready-made and just get the children involved at the rolling and cutting-out stage. If you have a large group, or don't want the mess of rolling out pastry, take the circles of dough ready-cut and each child can simply create his or her own smily face.

1. Cut small pieces of the butter into the flour.

2. Add sugar and, if using, ground nuts (or extra flour and cinnamon).

3. Rub mixture into 'crumbs' with your finger tips (or use a food processor).

4. Add the egg yolks and form the crumbs into dough (add a little milk if it is too dry).

5. Roll out pastry and cut out an even number of 6cm circles.

6. Make faces out of half the circles, by cutting out eyes with (washed) felt-pen lids. Use a pointed knife to cut out a smiling mouth.

7. Bake faces and plain bases on baking parchment in the pre-heated oven at 200°C for ten minutes, or until golden brown.

8. Gently warm the jam to make it easier to spread, and mix with the lemon juice. Spread the bases with jam and place a 'smiley' upon each jammy base.

9. With the aid of a tea strainer and teaspoon, sprinkle each face with a dusting of icing sugar.

(Makes about 30 biscuits)

Reproduced with permission from *Does Jesus Like Cake?* published by BRF 2003 (1 84101 319 6)

GOD ALWAYS LISTENS

- How do you think Jasmin felt about being called the Dustbin?
- If you had been in Robby's class, would you have joined in with the others against Jasmin?
- Have you ever felt the odd one out at school?
- Is it 'telling tales' to go to a teacher about these kind of problems at school? (Impress upon the children that it is absolutely necessary and very brave to tell an adult they can trust about bullying at school.)
- Think of a few words to describe what it might feel like to be bullied.

Bullying doesn't always mean hurting someone. It's all about how we treat other people, the way we speak to them and behave towards them. Do we care about making other people feel accepted and 'at home' or do we like getting into 'cliques' and keeping everyone else out of our little group?

Read Psalm 102:1–2 again. How do you think the person who wrote these words was feeling?

Sometimes, even people in the Bible felt far away from God. It's good to know that we can talk to him about those kinds of feelings. In what circumstances might we feel that God is hiding his face from us? In what ways can we know that he always listens when we pray?

Another psalm, Psalm 121, tells us that God is constantly watching over us, ready to help us when we need him. It says that he doesn't even need to sleep!

Where will I find help? It will come from the Lord, who created the heavens and the earth. The Lord is your protector, and he won't go to sleep or let you stumble. The protector of Israel doesn't doze or ever get drowsy... The Lord will protect you now and always wherever you go.
PSALM 121:1B–4, 8.

Whatever happens to us, we can talk to God about it, knowing that he will listen to us and watch over us.

TEASPOON PRAYER

Thanks: Thank you that we can talk to you about everything and that we can tell you how we are feeling, even about the worst things. Thank you that you listen and that you are always with us.

Sorry: (You can ask the children if they want to say sorry for ways in which they might have hurt other children, and leave a time of silence for them to do that.) Finish up with: Sorry that we haven't always treated others in the way that you would like us to.

Please: Please help us to be kind to other people and to remember that you love all of us.

A SONG TO SING

This song begins with a sentence spoken loudly and clearly by all the children: *'One thing's certain! All human beings need sleep!'*

Some people nod off quite quickly (children nod)
Some people have to count sheep (shout '2, 3, 4')
Some people breathe very thickly
(children breathe loudly)
Some people snore in their sleep (children snore)
Some people cuddle their teddies
(act cuddling teddy)
Some people toss, turn and lurch (children do so)
Some people sleep in their beddies
(children act sleeping)
Some people drop off in church (Amen)
(wake up with a jerk)

Chorus

But God never sleeps! He never slumbers!
He watches over us by day and night.
Whether we're sleeping, playing, eating, we're
Safe in the knowledge that he holds us tight.

Some people need clocks to wake up ('tick-tock')
Some people rise when it's light (children stretch)
Some people sleep in their make-up ('Yuk'!)
Some people dribble all night
(children wipe mouths)

Some people snooze with the box on
(children goggle)
Some people claim they just doze
(children make droopy eyes)
Some people leave both their socks on
(children hold noses)
Some people wriggle bare toes!
(children wriggle fingers)

Chorus

But God never sleeps! etc.

SOMETHING TO MAKE

A jelly baby asleep in a walnut-shell cradle is a good reminder to the children that, even when they are going through difficulties, they can sleep in peace because God, who never sleeps, is watching over them.

> **You need:**
> ☆ One half walnut shell per child (cut-up egg boxes or sea shells would be a possible substitute)
> ☆ Jelly babies (tell them not to eat the one in the cradle as it might get a bit gluey, but take enough extra ones for them to eat one each!)
> ☆ Enough glue for your group
> ☆ Felt scraps
> ☆ Cotton wool
> ☆ Scissors (one pair per child)

1. Cut out a piece of felt for the hood of the cradle, about 3cm by 7cm (depending on the size of the walnut shells).
2. Fold over lengthways and stick the two long ends together on one side. Stick this hood into the walnut shell.

3. Make padding for the jelly baby to lie on, by tearing off a bit of the cotton wool and placing it in the shell.

4. Place the jelly baby in the cradle and cover with a felt blanket, cut to the right size.

A GAME TO PLAY

Chinese whispers

For groups (or leaders) who don't like making things!

A game of 'Chinese whispers' illustrates the fact that although we don't always hear perfectly, God does. He never misunderstands what we say!

The children sit in a circle. Someone thinks of a silly sentence like 'My Dad snores when he sleeps'. That person whispers the sentence to the person on his or her right, and the message is then passed on through the whole group in whispers until it gets back to the person who originally started it. Inevitably, by the time the message has gone full circle, it has changed! The person who started repeats what s/he hears and then what the original message was.

The Snooze Song

'One thing's certain! All human beings need sleep!'

Some people nod off quite quickly (children nod)
Some people have to count sheep (shout '2, 3, 4')
Some people breathe very thickly (children breathe loudly)
Some people snore in their sleep (children snore)
Some people cuddle their teddies (act cuddling teddy)
Some people toss, turn and lurch (children do so)
Some people sleep in their beddies (children act sleeping)
Some people drop off in church (Amen) (wake up with a jerk)

But God never sleeps! He never slumbers!
He watches over us by day and night.
Whether we're sleeping, playing, eating, we're
Safe in the knowledge that he holds us tight.

Some people need clocks to wake up ('tick-tock')
Some people rise when it's light (children stretch)
Some people sleep in their make-up ('Yuk'!)
Some people dribble all night (children wipe mouths)
Some people snooze with the box on (children goggle)
Some people claim they just doze (children make droopy eyes)
Some people leave both their socks on (children hold noses)
Some people wriggle bare toes! (children wriggle fingers)

But God never sleeps! He never slumbers!
He watches over us by day and night.
Whether we're sleeping, playing, eating, we're
Safe in the knowledge that he holds us tight.

Reproduced with permission from *Does Jesus Like Cake?* published by BRF 2003 (1 84101 319 6)

Chapter 5

DOES JESUS LIKE CAKE?

As Jesus was teaching, he said: 'Guard against the teachers of the Law of Moses! They love to walk around in long robes and be greeted in the market. They like the front seats in the meeting places and the best seats at banquets. But they cheat widows out of their homes and pray long prayers just to show off. They will be punished most of all.'

Jesus was sitting in the temple near the offering box and watching people put in their gifts. He noticed that many rich people were giving a lot of money. Finally, a poor widow came up and put in two coins that were worth only a few pennies. Jesus told his disciples to gather round him. Then he said:

'I tell you that this poor widow has put in more than all the others. Everyone else gave what they didn't need. But she is very poor and gave everything she had. Now she doesn't have a penny to live on.'

MARK 12:38–44

Wrapped up in an apron that was much too big for her, Anna, her face aglow, was doing what she liked best. Arranged in front of her on the table was a neat row of saucers, each filled with a colourful heap of something delicious. There were sticky cherries, shiny Smarties, nuts, hundreds-and-thousands, silver balls and three different colours of icing. With the tip of her

tongue sticking out, Anna was concentrating hard on transforming each of the little cup cakes she had just baked with Granny into a work of art.

'Granny! I've finished,' she announced, licking her fingers as she proudly regarded the results of her handiwork. 'May I choose one now?' she begged. 'Just one! Not to eat now, I'm too full, but to take up to my room with me to eat before I go to sleep.'

Granny, her hands all soapy from the washing-up, came over to the kitchen table to have a look.

'You have done a good job, Anna!' she exclaimed. 'Whoever would have thought a five-year-old could decorate cakes so beautifully? I would be proud of those if I'd done them myself. But Anna, I need these cakes for our visitors tomorrow afternoon. It would be nice if everybody could have at least two cakes. Let's think who's coming.' Granny dried her hands on her apron and began counting on her fingers.

'There's Helen and Janet and Mrs P and maybe her daughter. Then there's the new couple from down the road, and it's possible that Robert and Doris might come. Work out for yourself if we've got enough.'

Now it was Anna's turn to put her freshly licked but still sticky fingers into action. She counted forwards and backwards but then gave up.

'I've run out of fingers,' she said with a sigh.

'Well, the recipe was supposed to make about eighteen cakes,' said Granny, 'but because quite a lot of the cake mixture somehow disappeared, we've only got fifteen. Now I'm not brilliant at maths, but if we have about eight guests, we need sixteen cakes—and if that sum is correct, then Grandpa is going to have to go without. Oh dear! Who's going to break the news to him, you or me?'

Anna understood at once that for the success of tomorrow afternoon, every single cake was necessary, but she was disappointed just the same. She had been so looking forward to the luscious combination of cherries, pink icing, Smarties and silver balls all held together by the fluffy golden cake in its pretty paper frill. Granny saw the expression on her face and hastily reconsidered, as grannies do.

'Mind you, I could just open a packet of biscuits, to boost them a bit,' she said slowly. 'And after all that hard work, you really should be allowed to taste one. Let's clear up, and then you can put on your pyjamas, and after your bedtime story you can choose one cake to take up with you. But I want a promise!'

'What's that?' asked Anna, leaping joyfully down from the chair where she had been perched for the baking.

'No crumbs in bed! And brush your teeth before you go to sleep.'

It didn't take Anna long to get ready, and after she had run outside to say goodnight to Grandpa, who was still busily working away in his workshop, she curled up on Granny's lap, freshly bathed and in her pyjamas.

'My story,' Granny began, 'is all about a widow who visited the temple while Jesus was teaching there. He was standing near the collecting boxes, and as he spoke to the crowds, rich and important people kept on coming over and throwing in their gifts of money. The jingle-jangle of coins made everyone look up to see who was giving so much. Then the old lady hobbled over. She was very poor and just put two small coins in the collection boxes. Clink, clink! They scarcely made a sound.'

'Just two?' asked Anna. 'That's not very much.'

Granny smiled. 'Jesus told his listeners that that old woman had put in more money than all the rich people,' she said.

'But only two coins!' cried Anna. 'Even I've got that much!'

'Jesus knew that those were her last two coins,' explained Granny. 'She gave God everything that she had. Those rich men who emptied their purses into the box probably had tons more money at home. They were just showing off. That widow gave her very last money—she wanted to give God everything.'

Granny shut her Bible and gave Anna a hug. 'It's getting late, Anna. Time for bed.'

'But what happened to the poor lady?' asked Anna.

'It doesn't tell us in the Bible exactly what happened to her after that,' said Granny. 'But as Jesus knew all that about her, you can be sure that she was in the best possible hands. Now jump down and go and choose your cake. Lights out in ten minutes and don't forget to brush your teeth. I'm just going to water the garden before it gets dark.'

And now Anna lay in bed, the most beautiful cake of all placed carefully next to her, on her bedside table. She had taken special trouble over this little cake. Right in the middle of the smooth pink icing she had placed a sticky red cherry surrounded by shiny silver balls, so that it looked like a flower. Anna's mouth began to water and she stretched out her hand to take the cake. As she looked at it from all sides, enjoying its perfection, she suddenly had an idea—an idea that gave her a little thrill of excitement, but at the same time cost her an inward struggle. The widow in the Bible had given her last money to God. How would it be if she, Anna, were to give this, her most beautiful cake, to Jesus? Slowly and thoughtfully, she put the cake back on the table. Then very quickly, before she could change her mind, she jumped out of bed, gave her teeth a quick clean, and then sprang back in again.

'Dear Lord Jesus,' she prayed. 'You can have my cake, if you want. I've made it look so beautiful and I really hope you will like it. Please take it if you want it. Amen.'

And then she lay there in the gathering darkness and hugged herself with joy. 'I wonder if I'll see him take it,' she said to herself before she fell asleep.

Anna was awakened next morning by the sun streaming through a gap in her curtains. Granny had such pretty, flowery curtains and for a while Anna just lay in bed, enjoying the way the sunlight made the colours of the material glow.

Suddenly she remembered yesterday evening and sat bolt upright in bed. She got a shock when she saw that the cake was still sitting on her bedside table, just as she had left it. Jesus had not eaten it—not even a cherry or a silver ball. A fly that had been eyeing it thoughtfully from the lampshade now buzzed over and landed on the pink icing. Quickly, Anna shooed it away, then picked up the cake. Although she was very disappointed, she suddenly felt that she had known all along that he wouldn't take it.

'Perhaps he doesn't need it,' she murmured. Then she couldn't resist it any longer. Carefully she tore off the paper case and took a small bite, allowing the glorious sweetness to melt in her mouth. Next she nibbled off a chewy cherry... It was the best cake she had ever eaten.

At breakfast that morning, Anna told Granny and Grandpa about giving her cake to Jesus. When she told them about her cake-prayer,

Grandpa spluttered, causing a mini-explosion in his coffee cup, and the white tablecloth was suddenly covered with a sprinkling of brown spots. Granny was smiling too, although at the same time her expression behind her glasses showed that she was taking Anna very seriously.

'That was a very nice idea of yours, Anna,' said Grandpa, blowing his nose loudly.

'Yes,' continued Granny, 'and I'm sure that Jesus understands what you meant and is pleased that you wanted to give him something that was worth so much to you. But Jesus isn't like us. He doesn't need to eat. He is almighty and powerful. He is great! He is... he is God.'

'Well, how can I please Jesus, then?' asked Anna. 'If he is too great for my cake, perhaps I'll only be able to please him when I'm a grown-up like you, and old. Then I can give him all my money.'

'It's just that Jesus sees things quite differently to the way we often do,' said Grandpa. 'He doesn't take so much notice of how the outside of things look. Wonderful clothes, or lots of money—things like that don't impress him, because he sees past the outside and looks straight at the inside. He knows our thoughts and what goes on in our hearts. Often it's the things that seem little and unimportant, like two small coins, or just making someone happy, which mean more than big, showy things.'

'Exactly,' said Granny, smiling. 'And that's why Grandpa is also now going to do something for Jesus, something seemingly little and un-important, but something that will help me, so that I have time to bake some more cakes with Anna...'

'What's that?' asked Grandpa, but already a look of horror was spreading over his face.

'The breakfast washing-up,' said Granny, 'followed by some tidying-up for our visitors.'

Anna knew that although Grandpa did such jobs obediently and thoroughly, he always liked to spend the mornings in his workshop.

'But why do we need more cakes?' she asked, delighted at the prospect but surprised at this sudden change of plans.

'Yesterday evening, after you had gone to bed,' said Granny, 'Grandpa came in from the workshop and found your cakes. Unfortunately,' (and here Granny laughed), 'I was out in the garden, doing the watering. When I came inside, there were seven cakes missing.'

By this time, Grandpa was already bending over the kitchen sink and clattering the cups and saucers. The back of his neck suddenly looked very red. Anna laughed and went over to the cupboard, where she got out the scales.

'It was 250g of butter and 250g of sugar, wasn't it, Granny?' was all she said.

Anna's cakes

★ Paper baking cases
★ 250g butter
★ 250g sugar
★ 4 eggs
★ 250g plain flour
★ 2 heaped teaspoons baking powder
★ 100g ground walnuts (can be omitted in the case of nut allergy, in which case add 50g extra flour)
★ Icing sugar
★ For lemon icing, the juice of one lemon
★ For coffee icing, 1 teaspoon instant coffee mixed with a little boiling water
★ Delicious things for decorating

At home, this is a simple and rewarding recipe to bake with children. For a group, it is better to restrict the activity to decorating only. Bake the cakes in advance and take enough for one or two per child. Divide the icing up into little containers and provide knives for spreading, plus plenty of different things for decorating (Smarties, hundreds-and-thousands and so on).

1. Cream together butter and sugar.

2. Mix in eggs, one at a time.

3. Add flour, baking powder and, if using, ground walnuts.

4. Put about a tablespoonful of the mixture in each baking case.

5. Bake at 180°C until a nice golden colour (about 15–20 minutes).

6. Make icing up to a nice thick consistency (always add liquid a little at a time to icing sugar, never the other way round, until you get the desired thickness).

7. Spread icing over cakes. The decorating needs to be done instantly, otherwise the icing goes hard and nothing sticks any more!

8. Before washing up, lick out the icing bowl thoroughly!

(Makes about 24 cakes.)

Reproduced with permission from *Does Jesus Like Cake?* published by BRF 2003 (1 84101 319 6)

APPEARANCES AND REALITY

You can find Anna's bedtime story in the Gospel of Mark. Can you imagine the scene? While Jesus was talking, lots of rich and important men were coming past and tossing their money into the collection box so that it made a lovely, loud, jangling noise. It was almost like a competition to see who could make the loudest jingle. If there was an especially loud jingle, then everyone would look up to see the rich and generous man who could afford to give the temple so much money. That man might then feel very pleased and proud of himself. He might even get all specially dressed up before he took his money to the temple, so that he really looked posh.

The ordinary people thought that these teachers looked so important as they paraded around, swooshing behind them the long, expensive robes they loved to wear. These men adored it when people stopped and stared at them on the streets or offered them the best seats in the synagogues. Often they would make a show of praying very long, loud, public prayers so that everyone would think, 'Oh, if only I could

be as good as them!' But Jesus told the crowd around him that although some of them looked and behaved like goodies on the outside, in reality they were baddies on the inside. He said that they sometimes greedily grabbed things that didn't belong to them from the poor people they were supposed to be looking after.

A GAME TO PLAY

Jingle-jangle

> You need:
> ☆ A cardboard box
> ☆ Different 'jangly' items to throw into it

Four children are chosen to throw 'money' into the box, and the rest are told to shut their eyes and listen carefully. They must try to guess who threw the most money in.

You can say something like, 'Has everyone got their eyes shut? OK, listen carefully, here comes Tom. What is he throwing into the offering box?'

The first child throws some toy cars into the box; the second, some marbles. The third offers a pound's worth of pennies and the fourth can let a

cheque for a hundred pounds (made out to yourself by yourself!) silently float into the box. (You can improvise as many different offerings as you want—for example, nails, potatoes and so on).

The children can guess each time what has been thrown in and at the end they can open their eyes and try to guess who has given the most.

After they've tried to guess, show them what was really thrown into the box. (You will need to explain the cheque.) Ask if the thing that made the most noise was worth the most.

When they all understand that the thing that made the least noise was actually worth the most, get them to think about things that 'make a lot of noise' today—things that are on TV or in the news-papers (for example, beautiful bodies, fashionable clothes, rich, famous people and so on).

Ask them what they think is more important—to wear the latest fashions and be 'cool', or to be kind and loving. Then draw their attention back to the 'offerings' in the box. Ask them again, which thing is worth the most?

Point out that for a multi-millionaire, to part with £100 is not a big deal. But there are some children in the poorer countries of this world for whom a handful of marbles or some toy cars represent untold wealth. To give away these treasured possessions to someone they love would be a real sacrifice.

Whether we are rich or poor has no bearing on doing things that please God. Christians believe that God knows what is going on in our hearts. The Bible tells us that we please him the most when we do things out of love for him.

TEASPOON PRAYER

Thanks: Thank you, Lord God, that we don't have to be special in any way to be your children. We don't need to be especially clever, especially rich, especially famous or especially good at anything.

Sorry: Sorry that we sometimes get in a muddle and think the unimportant things are important and forget about the things that really matter.

Please: Please help us to love you so that we can show your love to other people too.

A SONG TO SING

Jangle jingle, jingle jangle,
Sometimes life gets in a tangle,
Upside down and inside out.
Is that what life is all about?
Looking great and acting cool,
Getting brilliant marks at school,
Keeping up with all the trends,
Having fun and lots of friends…
Well, that's all right—it works for some—
But what about the lonely ones?
How people really feel inside,
That's something that they tend to hide.
But here's a truth for all who hurt,
Who don't fit in, who feel like dirt—
Jesus loves you! This we know
For the Bible tells us so!
It's more than cool, it outdoes smart,
To live with Jesus in your heart!

Get the kids to rap along to this. If they're into it, you can get some synchronized movement going and really work on it. You could even use a per-formance of it to wake up all the adults in church, after the sermon!

Chapter 6

GROWN-UPS CAN CRY TOO

'If you are tired from carrying heavy burdens, come to me and I will give you rest. Take the yoke I give you. Put it on your shoulders and learn from me, I am gentle and humble, and you will find rest. This yoke is easy to bear, and this burden is light.'

MATTHEW 11:28–30

Sometimes even grown-ups are so tired and fed-up that they feel like crying, as you will see in this story.

Granny had been on the phone for ages. At last she put down the receiver and turned to Anna and Grandpa.

'That was Rowena,' she said. 'You'll never guess what Jo-Jo's done now.'

Rowena was Granny's next-door neighbour, and Jo-Jo, her daughter, was nearly three.

'What?' asked Anna.

'Well, while she was supposed to be sitting on

51

her potty, Jo-Jo found a marker pen in the bathroom. She scribbled all over the lid and the seat of the toilet and, try as she might, Rowena just can't remove her daughter's artwork. Of course the seat is ruined.'

Grandpa chuckled. 'Jo-Jo's going through a creative phase!' he said.

'Anyway,' continued Granny, 'I offered to drive her to the shopping centre. There's a huge bathroom centre there and she needs to buy a new loo seat. Do you want to come, Anna?'

Half an hour later, Anna and Jo-Jo were perched in the back of Granny's car, while Jo-Jo's mum, Rowena, struggled with Jo-Jo's new little brother Thomas, who was screaming his head off.

'You can't be hungry, I've just fed you!' exclaimed Rowena, bundling him into his car seat. Jo-Jo put her hands to her ears to block out his screaming.

At last they were all strapped in, and as soon as Granny reached the bottom of the road, Thomas stopped bellowing and went to sleep.

'It's so kind of you to drive us,' said Rowena to Granny. 'We're going through a very difficult time at the moment. Jo-Jo is finding it very hard to adjust to being a big sister. When Tommy was born, she was very nearly potty-trained but she seems to have forgotten about potties now. She keeps wetting herself all over the place and

Tommy hardly ever stops crying and...' Then something terrible happened. Jo-Jo's mummy suddenly began to cry herself.

'I'm so sorry,' she sobbed. 'It just seems as though I'm always either feeding Tommy, while Jo-Jo gets into mischief, or wiping up Jo-Jo's puddles.'

Anna had never seen a grown-up cry before, apart from Mum. She felt dreadful and didn't know what to do.

'You must be worn out!' said Granny.

Rowena pulled out a hankie and blew her nose. 'I'm finding it hard coping on my own', she said. 'The nights are terrible!'

Anna really wanted to say something to help Rowena, but she couldn't think of anything at all. Then she had an idea.

'Granny,' she said. 'Jim-who-lives-downstairs says that the Bible is like a recipe book, with recipes for life in it. Are there any recipes about potty-training in the Bible?'

Granny smiled.

'Not directly about potty-training,' she said. 'But Jesus knows that we all sometimes feel completely worn-out and unable to cope, and there is a wonderful invitation in the Bible for everyone feeling like that.'

'How does it go?' asked Anna.

'It's in Matthew's Gospel, when Jesus says, "If you are tired from carrying heavy burdens, come to me and I will give you rest",' said Granny.

'And how does it work?' asked Anna.

'Well, you can tell Jesus all about your problems and ask him to help you,' answered Granny. 'Would you like me to do that with you, Rowena?'

'If you think it will do any good,' said Rowena, with a sniff.

So as she drove, Granny prayed out loud and asked God to give Rowena strength and encouragement. After that, Granny put on a tape, Rowena had a little snooze and Jo-Jo sucked her thumb. At last the shopping centre came into sight.

'Here we are,' said Granny. 'Oh good, there's even a space for us to park by the swings over there. I suggest we have a little something to eat first. Have you had any breakfast, Rowena?'

Rowena shook her head.

'Lucky I brought some food with me,' said

Granny over her shoulder, as she backed into a parking space. 'Pass my bag over, Anna.'

She stopped the car, rummaged around in the bag Anna reached her, and produced a flask of coffee, some sandwiches and a tin of home-made jammy biscuits.

After a delicious snack, during which Rowena cheered up a bit, they made their way through the slowly revolving glass doors and went up the escalator to the bathrooms department. Anna and Jo-Jo loved the way the shop people had built up lots of little bathrooms, each complete with a shiny washbasin and toilet and decorated with different coloured tiles. They wandered from one display room to the next, inspecting a family of rubber ducks and a fluffy towel with a dolphin on it, and smelling the different coloured soaps that were lying around. They found some soap that looked so much like strawberries that Jo-Jo stuck one in her mouth and then spat it out in disgust, for it tasted horrible.

'Which bathroom would you like in your house, Jo-Jo?' asked Anna.

'That red one,' said Jo-Jo, pointing at a bright, shiny red washbasin surrounded by white tiles with big red flowers on them. The toilet was red too, but with a white seat which was lavishly splattered with the same red flowers as were on the tiles.

Anna looked round to see which bathroom she liked the best. When she turned back, she was most surprised to see Jo-Jo with her trousers round her ankles, waddling straight to the lovely shiny toilet and heaving herself on to the seat.

'I need to do a wee-wee,' she announced.

'Oh, Jo-Jo, I don't think…' began Anna, looking round in desperation for Granny, Rowena and baby Thomas. But they were nowhere to be seen. 'Wait a moment, Jo-Jo,' she said. 'I'll just get your mummy!'

Anna ran through the maze of little bathrooms in a panic. She knew that all those spick-and-span arrangements were only there for people to look at, not for people to actually use. But Jo-Jo was only small. She didn't understand that. Oh, where was Granny? At last, rounding a corner, she found Granny and Rowena inspecting a row of toilet seats, hanging on a wall. She ran up and tugged at Granny's hand.

'Oh, there you are, Anna,' she said. 'Where's Jo-Jo?'

Before Anna could answer they heard Jo-Jo's voice, singing loudly:

'Mummy, Mummy,
I've finished on the potty.
Mummy, Mummy,
Come and wipe my botty!'

'Oh no!' cried Rowena. 'Has she wet herself again?'

'No—she's used the red loo with the flowers,' whispered Anna.

Rowena looked at her for a moment, her face a blank.

'Where is she?' she asked, clutching baby Thomas and looking panic-stricken.

It took Anna a while to find her way back to the bathroom showroom with the red flowers because all the little rooms leading in and out of one another were most confusing. But Jo-Jo cheerfully continued to sing her song, so they followed the sound of her voice. By the time they found her, quite a little crowd had gathered around, a circle of people staring, pointing, laughing. A few children were holding their noses and fanning the air while they shrieked and giggled. Rowena looked as though she was going to start crying again, but Jo-Jo, enthroned like a queen, beamed when she saw her mother.

'Look, Mummy, this time I've done it on the loo!' she announced loudly and proudly. A shop assistant came hurrying forward, looking rather angry. In his hand he clutched a spray bottle and he kept jerking down his finger and ejecting little jets of a sickly-smelling scent. His face looked so cross that Anna closed her eyes.

'Oh help!' she prayed. 'Please help!'

The shop assistant cleared his throat and opened his mouth to speak, but before he could say anything, Anna did something very brave. She ran forward and said very fast, with all her words tumbling over one another and her knees feeling rather trembly, 'Please can I tell you a secret?'

The shop assistant was so surprised that he obediently bent down and Anna whispered in his ear.

'Please don't be cross! My granny will help clear it up. But Jo-Jo's used the loo for the first time and she's so pleased with herself. If you're cross, it will spoil everything!'

He must have had children of his own. His face cleared and he stood up.

'Ladies and gentlemen!' he announced to the little knot of people gathered around Jo-Jo. 'May I announce that this young lady has, for the very first time, used the loo! On behalf of the bathrooms department I would like to say how delighted we are that for this momentous occasion in her young life she has picked our exclusive design, "Poppies". In my capacity as manager, I would like to give her as a gift the seat upon which she is now sitting as a memory of her first time in the right place.'

Rowena gasped, Granny grinned and Anna did a little skip for joy.

A little later they were all strapped into the car again, Granny and Rowena laughing in the front with the three children in the back, Jo-Jo clutching her new, flowery loo seat. Proudly, she stuck her dark, curly head through the hole in the middle and hung the seat round her neck with the lid sticking out at the back.

Jammy whammies

1. Mix together flour, sugar and (if using) ground nuts.

2. Add butter, in small cubes. Rub butter into dry ingredients.

☆ 200g butter
☆ 100g sugar
☆ 2 egg yolks
☆ 300g flour
☆ 100g ground hazelnuts (optional—use 50g more flour if omitting nuts)
☆ 1/2 cup icing sugar
☆ 150g redcurrant jelly

3. Add egg yolks and mix to make a dough. Form the dough into small balls.

4. Make an indentation in each ball with the end of a wooden spoon.

5. Line a baking tray with baking paper and bake at 200°C for 12–15 minutes.

6. When baked, allow to cool, then sprinkle the icing sugar over the biscuits using a tea strainer and a teaspoon.

7. Warm up the redcurrant jelly and fill each indentation with it.

8. Leave the biscuits out overnight, well away from insects or pets, for the jam to dry before storing the 'jammy whammies' in a tin.

(Makes about 60 biscuits.)

Reproduced with permission from *Does Jesus Like Cake?* published by BRF 2003 (1 84101 319 6)

OPEN INVITATION

You need:
- ☆ A few articles of clothing (scarves, hats, blouse, and so on)
- ☆ A hand mirror
- ☆ A white paper bag for everyone in the group
- ☆ A big heap of stones to represent our problems (or potatoes, building blocks and so on).
- ☆ A good sense of humour and the willingness to try to do a little acting!

Be prepared to let the children interact and don't be afraid to deviate from your script if they raise other issues.

Ask the children:

'Do you like getting invitations? What kind of things do you get invited to? I'm very excited— I got an invitation today. I've got it in my pocket. Would you like to get an invitation like this?'

Pull the invitation out of your pocket and read:

'Come to my birthday party! We are going to have so much fun! There'll be fireworks, cake and presents for everyone! Hope you can make it!

'Bet you wish you could go to a party like that. I can't wait. I wonder what I should wear.'

Do a bit of acting. Take several articles of clothing with you. Try them on or hold them against you. Ask the children which they think look better. Worry about which make-up/aftershave to wear, or whether the hat clashes with your shoes. Maybe you should splash out on a new outfit? Then begin to say things like:

'Well, I'd better get a move on, I might be late. I wonder if I should take a taxi, or go by foot. What would you do? Do you know how far away it is? How much time have I got before I have to leave?'

As you say this, keep reading through the invitation out loud and try to get the children to point out to you that:

- It doesn't say who the invitation is from.
- It doesn't say where the party is.
- It doesn't say what day the party is.
- It doesn't say what time the party is.

When all that has been established, say something like:

'But of course, how silly of me. That was the wrong pocket. Let's see—I know there's another one in there somewhere.'

Pull it out and read:

'Come to my birthday party! When? *(read yesterday's date)* Where? At No. 3 Abbots Road. What time? Four o' clock. We are going to have so much fun! There'll be fireworks, cake and presents for everyone! Hope you can make it! Lots of love, Joe Bloggs.

'Oh wonderful! Now, do you think I'll make that by foot, or should I take a taxi? Four o'clock—good, still a bit of time to get ready… I do love fireworks… And presents for everyone…'

Go on like this until the children point out to you (or if they don't realize, suddenly notice yourself) that the party is already over. You have missed it. Act very crestfallen.

'Oh my goodness! The party was yesterday. Oh, how sad! What a shame! They had fireworks, cake and presents and I wasn't there. I've missed everything. It's all over.

'Oh dear. That's the trouble with most invitations. They are only valid for a certain amount of time and if you miss the date, then you've missed the party. But that's not the case with the invitation we heard about today in the story. Can anyone remember it?

'Jesus says, "Come to me, all you who are weary and burdened and I will give you rest." Who is that invitation for? Christians believe it's for anyone who is feeling worried, sad, tired, or ill.

'Does the invitation only count until a certain date? No, it's for whenever we're feeling weary or burdened.

'Do we have to go to a special place for the invitation? No, Christians believe we can talk to Jesus and tell him about how we're feeling wherever and whenever we feel like it.

'And are there any conditions to this invitation? Do we have to bring something along? No, it's absolutely free.

'And if we accept the invitation and take along all our cares and troubles and ask Jesus for his help, what do we get? The Bible says that he will give us rest.

'What kind of things can make us feel weary and burdened? Do you have any ideas?'

Give each child a white paper bag. On the bag they can write (or have written) their suggestions.

When they have written down all their burdens on the bag, tell them to go to the pile of stones and for each problem they have written down, they should put a stone in their bag.

Then tell the children to pick up their bags and sling them over their shoulders and march around the room with them. Then say something like:

'Well, we have a choice. We can either choose to carry around our problems ourselves, or we can choose to accept the invitation in the Bible and take them to Jesus. That's what I'm going to do with mine.'

You can show the children how you empty out your stones. Then sing or read the following song.

A SONG TO SING

We bring to you, O Lord,
The things we're going through,
Our tears, our cares, our fears,
We bring them all to you.
Help us to hold your hand,
For yoked with you we know
That we will have your peace.
Please never let us go.

(The tune of the next part of this song fits above the tune of the first part, like a descant.)

Rest for the weary
Is very near.
When things get dreary,
Jesus is here.
He says, 'Come to me
All you who seek...
You'll find rest through me,
Strength for the weak.'

Teach the children the song. They can empty their stones out as they sing it. At the end they can blow up their empty bags and pop them to symbolize what happens when we accept the invitation not to carry our burdens around with us.

TEASPOON PRAYER

Thanks: Dear Lord, you didn't say that if we followed you we wouldn't have any problems, but thank you that you never leave us alone with our burdens. Thank you that you help us to carry them, so the load is lighter.

Sorry: Sorry for the many times when we try to muddle through on our own and forget to talk to you about our difficulties.

Please: Please show us how we can help other people who are in trouble.

Rest for the Weary

We bring to you, O Lord,
The things we're going through,
Our tears, our cares, our fears,
We bring them all to you.
Help us to hold your hand,
For yoked with you we know
That we will have your peace.
Please never let us go.

Rest for the weary
Is very near.
When things get dreary,
Jesus is here.
He says, 'Come to me
All you who seek...
You'll find rest through me,
Strength for the weak.'

Reproduced with permission from *Does Jesus Like Cake?* published by BRF 2003 (1 84101 319 6)

Chapter 7

THERE'S NO SUCH THING AS USELESS

> *The Lord told me, 'Go to the pottery shop, and when you get there, I will tell you what to say to the people.' I went there and saw the potter making clay pots on his pottery wheel. And whenever the clay would not take the shape he wanted, he would change his mind and form it into some other shape.*
>
> JEREMIAH 18:1–4

Wednesday afternoon, rounders, and it was Samantha Archer's turn. Anxiously, Andy counted the people in front of him. Two more, then it would be his turn. Samantha hit the ball and ran to second base. Now it was Derek Carter. Derek stood with the rounders bat clenched dangerously in his hand. Nippi Visram, who was bowling, took a step backwards, then raised his hand. Derek's body stiffened, his arm reached back, and whack! The ball sailed over the heads of the furthest fielders. His team went mad.

'Rounder! Rounder!' they chanted gleefully.

Casually Derek ambled round the pitch while the fielders raced after the ball. A burst of applause greeted him as he got past the fourth post.

'Seven to eight! Now it's all up to you, Andy!'

Andy stepped forward. He hated that feeling of loneliness, of being set apart from all the rest, that always overcame him when it was his turn to step on to that worn, grassy patch to hit the hard little rounders ball. He already knew what was going to happen. Miserably he waited for the humiliating moment. Behind him he heard a voice say, 'Mr Darlington, can't we have someone else to hit the ball? He always misses it. It's not fair having him on our team!'

Nippi poised himself to bowl.

'Come on, Andy!' boomed Mr Darlington. 'You could at least look as though you're trying!'

Andy gritted his teeth. Of course he was trying! The ball came hurtling towards him. He swung out with the bat and felt that desperate surge of longing for the nice cracking sound that should follow. As always, the ball thudded harmlessly to the ground and his team groaned. The others tittered. Hurriedly he made for first base.

'Drop the bat!' shrieked his team. He dropped it just as the ball went whizzing past his ear and into the hands of the girl on first base. At least he was out and wouldn't have to go through the torture again. He turned to go and sit on the edge of the rounders pitch.

'Not so fast, Andy!' roared Mr Darlington. 'You just need to try harder! Now, you're going to have another three bowls and for every one you miss, your team will get a rounder cancelled out.'

Andy could hardly believe his ears. There was a short silence, followed by a loud outburst of protest from his team. Bright red in the face, Andy turned and took up his position again.

Three misses later, his cheeks burning, Andy sat in the long grass and watched the insects scurrying through the jungle of blades.

*

'I hate Mr Darlington!' announced Andy, when he got home that day. He slammed his school bag down hard. It slithered over the floorboards and crashed into the radiator, bursting open and spewing a pile of exercise books, scrumpled up chocolate papers and pencil-sharpenings all over the floor. Mum looked up from the sewing machine.

'For heaven's sake, Andy!' she said crossly. 'Pick that up! Oh! Now look what you've made me do!' And there was a grinding snap as the sewing machine's needle broke in half. 'Oh, that's all I need,' she groaned. 'I'm late already, but I just had to mend the tear in this dress. I need it for the concert tonight.' She started to talk to the sewing machine. 'Come on—please go through.' She threaded a new needle and the machine hummed busily again. Finished at last, Mum grabbed the dress, folded it and put it in the little black case she used for concerts.

'I've got to go now,' she said. 'I should have left half an hour ago. Jim's looking after you lot, Andy. Go and find him and tell him I'm leaving now.' She grabbed a piece of cake, stuffed it in her mouth and picked up her cello in one hand and her case in the other. 'Open the door, please!' she ordered through the cake.

Andy went down to see Jim. Jim was baking bread. He was just kneading out the dough, folding it over, punching it down. His strong arms worked tirelessly. Andy watched. Jim grinned at him in greeting.

'How was school?' he asked. 'Judging by the way you banged the door just now, it wasn't too good. Funny, last Wednesday too, I was down here doing my bread and you gave the door a bash like that. Is there something about Wednesdays you don't like?'

Andy gaped. Jim noticed everything. Slowly he began to talk about Mr Darlington and rounders.

'I just felt so useless,' he finished. 'I still do. I hate being me. In fact, I wish I were dead.'

Jim paused in his kneading. 'Give your hands a wash, could you?' he said. 'I could do with some help here.'

Glumly, Andy obeyed. Jim gave him a piece of dough.

'Just roll this out into a long shape, like a snake, but nice and even,' he said. Andy rolled the dough out into a long sausage.

'That's great,' said Jim. He took the long coil and broke it into six shorter pieces. Deftly and swiftly he plaited three of them into a neat braided roll. Then he took the next three strands of dough. 'Now, watch this,' he said. This time the strands of dough got into a tangle and the result was a mess. Jim scratched his head, leaving a smear of flour on his cheek.

'Oh no!' he said. 'That one's rubbish! I'll have to throw it down the toilet.' And he picked up the heap of dough and made as if to throw it in the direction of the bathroom.

'Don't!' cried Andy. 'You can knead the dough and use it again!'

'Of course I can,' said Jim, doing so very fast indeed, so that a perfect little braided roll was plopped on to the baking sheet next to its brother. 'So can you, you know.'

'What do you mean?' asked Andy.

'Well, you're just like this dough. When something goes wrong, you can make a few adjustments and try again. And those arms, legs and eyes of yours are very good at other things, even if they're not the best at hitting rounders balls. Who got fifty out of fifty in the spelling test last week?'

Andy considered. That was true. He was good at spelling. He just didn't seem to have to try. Poor Derek Carter had had to do the test again.

'I've got enough rolls now,' said Jim. He gave Andy a pastry brush and together they painted each roll with beaten egg and then sprinkled black poppy seeds on top. Jim carried the two baking trays over to the stove to rise. Andy admired their handiwork. The rolls were laid out in perfect rows, each a tiny work of art.

'There's one bit of dough left over,' said Jim. 'Tell you what, let's get a bit of rounders practice in.' For a moment Andy didn't know what he meant, until he suddenly found himself positioned in the middle of Jim's kitchen, clutching the rolling pin in his hand, while Jim, with a flourish, bowled the last soft, round ball of dough in his direction. Andy lunged out and SLAP! the dough landed stickily on the rolling pin, then dropped to the floor.

'Bull's eye!' yelled Jim. 'Oh yes! That would have been half a rounder at least. Let's try again.'

Very soon the dough was a grimy grey colour, with specks of dirt sticking to it. Sometimes it landed on the floor, but sometimes Andy gave it a whack. Once he sent it into the sink. After some successful shots, Jim went over to see if the other rolls had risen.

'Look at that,' he said. 'We tried our best to make them all the same, but each one's just a bit different. That one there has risen more—it looks all puffy. That one there has got its end pointing up. That one is a bit squashed where your rounders ball landed on it, and that one has got a crack in the middle. Hand-made, each one unique, each one special in its own way. Just like you and me, really.'

Poppy-seed plaits

★ 500g strong white flour
★ 7g dried yeast
★ 250ml warm water
★ 1 teaspoon salt
★ For decorating: 1/2 cup poppy seeds, 1 beaten egg mixed with a little salt

1. Mix flour and yeast together thoroughly and add warm water.

2. Mix to a firm but springy consistency, adding a little more water if necessary. Knead well.

3. Leave to rise for about half an hour in a covered bowl. Knead again and divide the dough into 50g portions.

4. Divide each portion into three and roll out three 'sausages'. Use these to plait braids. (Of course the children do not have to make braids but can form the dough in any way they wish.)

5. Place rolls on baking sheets lined with baking paper. Leave space between each roll, as they 'grow' a lot in the oven. (On the baking paper, you can make sure each child gets his or her own handiwork by marking and naming 'territory' with a pencil.)

6. Brush each braid with egg and sprinkle with poppy seeds.

7. Place an ovenproof dish with water in the oven and preheat on 220°C.

8. Allow the rolls to rise for another 15 minutes and then bake for 10–15 minutes. Eat warm with plenty of butter.

(Makes about 15 rolls.)

EACH ONE OF US IS UNIQUE AND SPECIAL

You need three photos of yourself:
☆ As a baby
☆ As a child
☆ A recent photo

It might also be helpful to have a selection of different pottery items—vases, jugs and mugs of various shapes and sizes.

Hold up picture no. 1. Say, 'Here's a picture of a lovely little baby that you all know. Just in case you're not sure who it is, I'll give you a clue.'

Hold up picture no. 2. Say, 'This is the same person. Any ideas who it could be?'

Hold up picture no. 3. Say, 'Did you recognize me?'

Hold all three pictures up and ask the children for ways in which you have changed. Talk about yourself as a child. Mention any things you used to be bad at but can do now. Did you hate vegetables? Did you like having to have a rest after lunch? Wouldn't you just love to be able to do that now?

Point out that each person changes so much. Each person contains so much potential, we have so many gifts that we can use. What are some of the things that the children are good or bad at?

The following verses come from the book of Jeremiah in the Old Testament. Jeremiah reports:

The Lord told me, 'Go to the pottery shop, and when you get there, I will tell you what to say to the people.' I went there and saw the potter making clay pots on his pottery wheel. And whenever the clay would not take the shape he wanted, he would change his mind and form it into some other shape.

JEREMIAH 18:1–4

Jeremiah was a prophet. That means that God spoke very clearly to him and he passed on God's words to the people of Israel. One day, God told Jeremiah to go down to the house of the local potter. Do you know what a potter is? He uses clay and a potter's wheel to make beautiful pots for carrying water, for cooking and eating food, and for keeping things in. There are never two handmade pots exactly the same. Some are tall and slender, some are short and fat. Some make beautiful vases, some make lovely jugs, some are ideal for keeping the honey in. All of them are very useful and very attractive.

Jeremiah was used to seeing potters at work. Pots were always being made—they were used a lot, as there was no plastic alternative in those days. But this time, the potter forming the clay became a picture for Jeremiah of the way God can mould and form us, transforming each one of us into a unique, useful and beautiful person. Like the potter's pots, we each look different, and are good at different things. When things go wrong, God doesn't leave us alone. He can re-form us, reshape us, help us to change, like a potter can re-form a lump of clay into a beautiful and useful pot.

So don't give up! And don't forget, even if you

are bad at something, like Andy was at rounders, there are still lots of other things that you are good at. They might not be school things. Maybe you are good at being kind to other people, or good at playing the recorder. All those things are important and go to make up the very unique person you are. And you can try to remember all the things you are good at while, together with God, you work at the things that still need a bit of kneading and shaping.

Have you ever heard of one of Jesus' special friends, Peter, his disciple? Peter was a very impulsive person and there are lots of occasions we can read about in the Bible when he made embarrassing mistakes and really made a fool of himself. This clumsy fisherman often sank into the depths of despair when he put his foot in it yet again. But he didn't give up. He loved Jesus and because of that he kept going. Who would have thought that one day he would turn into such a powerful preacher that thousands of people came to know Jesus through him?

We are the clay, you are the potter; we are all the work of your hand.

ISAIAH 64:8 (NIV)

TEASPOON PRAYER

Thanks: Thank you, Lord Jesus, for the fantastic way in which each of us has been made.

Sorry: Sorry for when we spoil the design you made us in by doing wrong things.

Please: Please help us when things go wrong…

A GAME TO PLAY

Crazy dough

You need:
- ☆ Enough playdough for each group playing to have a good-sized lump. (It is cheap and easy to make your own playdough. See recipe that follows.)
- ☆ A list of things that the children can easily form with the playdough—for example, dog, person, apple, car, sausage, snail, butterfly, elephant, banana, horse, ball, boat, mouse, and so on.

Divide the children into groups of about five.

One person from each group comes to the group leader (who is standing at an equal distance from each group in the middle of the room. With big groups, you might need to use two or three leaders all armed with the same list). Each person is told the word at the top of the list—for example, 'a dog'.

They have to run back to their groups and try to form the object they have been told out of

playdough, without saying a word. The other group members have to guess what the child is trying to make. He or she is only allowed to answer 'yes' or 'no' to their suggestions. As soon as someone has guessed correctly, that person has to run to the group leader and get the next word on the list. The first group to get through the whole list wins.

RECIPE FOR PLAYDOUGH

☆ 2 cups flour
☆ 1 cup salt
☆ 2 tablespoons oil
☆ 4 teaspoons cream of tartar
☆ About 2 cups water
☆ Food colouring

1. Mix all ingredients together, adding a little water at a time.
2. Cook over a low heat for about five minutes. Stir constantly until the mixture leaves the side of the pan.
3. Remove from heat, and colour with food colouring by working it into the dough with your hands.

The dough will last for at least two weeks. To prevent it from drying out, keep in an airtight container in the fridge until needed.

Chapter 8

HAMMERSMITH RISES TO THE CHALLENGE

(AN EASTER STORY)

This is how John speaks of Jesus at the beginning of his Gospel.

> *Everything that was created received its life from him, and his life gave light to everyone. The light keeps shining in the dark, and the darkness has never put it out...*
>
> *The true light that shines on everyone was coming into the world. The Word was in the world, but no one knew him, though God had made the world with his Word. He came into his own world, but his own nation did not welcome him. Yet some people accepted him and put their faith in him. So he gave them the right to be the children of God.*

JOHN 1:3B–5, 9–12

Now sit down like a good boy and eat your porridge,' said Mum.

'I don't like porridge! Nasty porridge!' shrieked the baby and threw his bowl on the floor.

'Now look what a mess you've made,' scolded Mum. As she bent down to pick it up, a large, furry snout appeared round the kitchen door.

'Help! A monster!' screamed Mum, snatching up the baby and running over to the sink...

Anna was playing with her doll's house. She made the mother doll tremble and scream, and squeezed and bent her pipe-cleaner arms so that she could hold the baby doll. The 'monster' drew nearer, snuffling inquisitively round the kitchen. He wasn't really a monster at all, but Hammersmith, Robby's pet hamster, who often paid a visit to the family of dolls.

'Don't worry, Mum!' said the little boy doll, with Robby's voice. 'I can tame the monster!' Robby wrapped the boy doll's hands around a sunflower seed and waved it in front of Hammersmith's nose.

'Careful!' moaned the mother doll. 'He'll gobble you up!'

But Hammersmith took the sunflower seed and tucked it gratefully into one of his cheek pouches, which was already bulging with all the other titbits he was picking up. His career as a monster was proving to be very profitable.

'Robby! Anna!' called their real mother from the kitchen. 'Look outside! It's starting to snow! Snow in March—that's unbelievable!'

Robby and Anna looked up from where they were lying spread out on the floor in front of the doll's house.

'How strange,' said Robby, jumping up and putting Hammersmith back in his cage on the windowsill. He opened the window to look out into the leaden grey sky. Great white flakes were floating down. 'No snow at Christmas, but a white Easter—weird!'

'Maybe we'll have to look for Easter eggs in the snow tomorrow,' said Anna happily, for tomorrow was Easter Day, and after lunch their church always organized an egg-hunt in the nearby park.

'Come on, let's go outside and catch snowflakes!' suggested Robby, and they rushed off to get into their boots, hats, scarves and mittens as quickly as possible. They were so eager to get outside that Robby completely forgot to shut the window.

That evening, when Robby went to feed Hammersmith, he had a terrible shock. The hamster was in his bed of wood shavings and shredded paper, but he was stretched out, stiff and cold. His fur was all rumpled up the wrong way. When Robby picked him up, he did not move. There was something very wrong. Mum came running at the sound of Robby's shouts and confirmed his worst suspicion.

'I think Hammersmith is dead,' she said, putting her arm round Robby and hugging him. Robby was too stunned even to cry.

∗

Easter Day was bright and sunny, even though it was very cold and there had been a light scattering of frost in the morning. Robby knelt on a chair at the window, his nose pressed against the glass, his hands resting on Hammersmith's empty cage. Last night he had cried himself to sleep and this morning he had been unable to enjoy the boiled eggs with faces painted on them that Mum had made for breakfast. In church he had listened to the Easter story and understood the absolute despair that Jesus' friends had felt as Jesus' lifeless, helpless body was shut away in the burial cave, sealed up with a large, heavy rock placed at the opening.

Why did Jesus have to die? And Hammersmith? His stiff little body was lying in a box in the greenhouse. In a few minutes they would bury him in the garden. Robby had already dug a hole, together with Dad. Through the window, he saw Dad walking towards the greenhouse. Robby ran down to join him. He wanted to say goodbye.

The sun was beating down on the glass panels of the greenhouse and everything was drenched in its warm, golden light. Although it was crisp and cold outside, inside the greenhouse it was warm and smelt damp and earthy. The seeds that Mum had planted had already shot up and produced little green leaves, which were straining their necks to suck in as much sunshine as possible. Hammersmith was stretched out in his box, lit up by a shaft of sunlight. Above his motionless little body, dust particles were weaving in and out of an endless dance. Robby put his hand into the box, scooped up Hammersmith and gently stroked him, while Dad put his arm round his shoulders.

'Do animals go to heaven, Dad?' asked Robby, quietly.

'That's a difficult question, Robby,' answered Dad. 'I must admit, I don't really know the answer.'

At that moment, something unbelievable happened. Hammersmith gave a tiny twitch. It was so tiny that Robby thought he must be imagining things. He stroked the rumpled fur again. This time there was no mistaking it. Hammersmith definitely moved.

'Dad!' gasped Robby. 'Something's happening!'

*

The whole family was assembled in the kitchen, listening to the voice of Mr Simpson, the vet, on the phone. In spite of it being Easter Sunday, Mum had rung him.

'Yes, yes,' he was saying cheerfully, his mouth obviously still full with his Easter Sunday roast, 'it often happens that hamsters can go into hibernation if there is a sudden drop in temperature. The breathing rate slows so that it is scarcely detectable and they simply save on food and energy by going into a deep sleep to get them through the winter. I expect quite a few pets have been buried alive by their sorrowing owners, but yours was lucky, wasn't he? Just keep him nice and warm and he'll be as right as rain. Happy Easter to you all! Goodbye.'

Hammersmith was sitting somewhat groggily in Robby's hand. His bright, beady little eyes were open and his fur was all pointing in the right direction again. Robby drew a deep breath.

'He's alive!' he said triumphantly. 'How amazing—on Easter Day!'

'Do you think that happened to Jesus too?' asked Anna. 'I mean that he wasn't really dead, but just asleep?'

'No,' said Robby, who had been listening carefully in church that morning. 'Jesus was nailed to the cross and then the soldiers stuck a spear in his side to make sure he was really dead. Then his body was put in a cave and a really heavy stone was rolled in front of the opening to stop anyone going in or coming out. One person couldn't have moved it on their own. But wow, now I can really imagine what a surprise Jesus' friends got when they found the stone had been rolled away and that the tomb was empty. They must have been completely gobsmacked when they saw him again.'

'Hammersmith will really die one day,' said Dad, gently stoking the hamster with his large finger. 'And so will we all. But because of what Jesus did for us on the cross at Easter, death is not the end. If we believe in Jesus, after we die our spiritual selves live on for ever and ever. We have life with Jesus.'

Resurrection rocks

Eating these scrumptious, squidgy, chocolate-covered choux pastry 'rocks' together can be a celebration of the fact that the heavy stone used to seal Jesus' tomb was removed and the grave was empty.

There are two ways of using this recipe for a group of children.

☆ The choux buns can be made beforehand and simply filled and covered with chocolate by the children.

☆ The pastry can be brought along and the children can put dollops of it on the baking sheet with a spoon. The rocks can bake while the story is being told. The fact that they rise a good deal can also be used to underline the resurrection theme.

> ☆ 250ml water
> ☆ 60g butter
> ☆ 200g plain flour
> ☆ 4 eggs
>
> **Filling:** Either 250ml whipped cream with 3 teaspoons sugar, or vanilla sauce made with 40g custard powder, 3 tablespoons sugar, a few drops vanilla essence and 500ml milk.
>
> **Topping:** 250ml cream and a few squares of cooking chocolate

1. Pre-heat the oven to 230°C. (It is very important that the pastry blobs are placed in a really hot oven, otherwise they will not rise properly.)

2. Boil up the water and butter in a large, roomy saucepan.

3. When the water is boiling and the butter has melted, tip in all the flour and stir until the flour-and-water mixture forms a large dumpling.

4. Place the dough in a bowl and add the eggs one at a time, using an electric mixer to incorporate each one thoroughly before adding the next.

5. Run the tap over the ungreased baking sheet and, leaving drops of water on it, place about 14 spoonfuls of dough on the sheet, leaving plenty of space between each one.

Reproduced with permission from *Does Jesus Like Cake?* published by BRF 2003 (1 84101 319 6)

6. When the oven has reached the required temperature, sprinkle a little water on to the base of the oven and quickly place the baking tray into it before the steam subsides. (The steam helps the rising process.)

7. Close the oven door and do not be tempted to open it for the next 15 minutes, otherwise the rocks will turn into flops!

8. Bake for 20–25 minutes. When they have risen and are golden brown, turn off the oven but leave the rocks inside, with the oven door propped slightly open, for another ten minutes or so. This ensures that they will not sink.

9. Take out the rocks, wait for them to cool, then slit open with a sharp knife. Fill either with whipped cream (naughty but nice) or with vanilla sauce (slightly more calorie-conscious, but still delicious).

10. To make topping, heat up the cream and chocolate in a small saucepan. Bring to the boil, stirring vigorously. Allow to cool a little, then coat each 'resurrection rock' with chocolate.

(Makes about 14 cakes)

Reproduced with permission from *Does Jesus Like Cake?* published by BRF 2003 (1 84101 319 6)

DARKNESS AND LIGHT

You need:
★ Some normal birthday candles
★ Some 'everlasting' birthday candles
 (the kind that keep on relighting after they
 have been blown out)

John writes in his Gospel that the coming of Jesus into this world is a little bit like suddenly bringing blazing light into a very dark place. Perhaps you can remember a time when you have woken up in the middle of the night and been very scared by the blackness all around you? What's the sensible thing to do at a moment like that? Switching on the light makes everything safe and cosy again, doesn't it? What a big contrast there is between light and darkness! Let's write down a few words about light and darkness. Can you help me to think of some?

Gather ideas to illustrate the two concepts of light and darkness. For example:

Light	Darkness
• Bright	• Black
• You can see	• You can't see
• Glowing	• Scary
• Safe	• Dangerous
• Enables you to move about without bumping into things	• Could be nasty things lurking about

In the Bible, John says that Jesus is like light and that the world without him is in darkness.

Everything that was created received its life from him, and his life gave light to everyone. The light keeps shining in the dark, and the darkness has never put it out...

The true light that shines on everyone was coming into the world. The Word was in the world, but no one knew him, though God had made the world with his Word. He came into his own world, but his own nation did not welcome him. Yet some people accepted him and put their faith in him. So he gave them the right to be the children of God.

JOHN 1:3B–5, 9–12

Jesus said of himself: 'I am the light for the world! Follow me, and you won't be walking in the dark. You will have the light that gives life' (John 8:12).

At this point, light a candle and ask the children if they can blow it out. Allow them to blow it out a few times. Then ask them if they can switch the

light on or off, and get them to do that a few times. Then ask them if it is possible to switch off the light of the world, Jesus. Ask them if anyone ever tried to switch him off. Point out that the people who crucified Jesus thought that using brutal force and killing him would put a stop to him for ever. They tried to switch off the light of the world, but it didn't work.

Light the everlasting candle and let the children try to blow it out. It should spark into life after every attempt to blow it out. This is just a tiny picture of how Jesus' light was too strong even for death. He rose again and is alive today. He loves each one of us and wants to bring his bright light into each of our lives and save us from living in darkness.

That's what the song today is about.

A SONG TO SING

I can (*) switch the light off!
(At * make the sound of the light switch
by clicking fingers)
With the flick of a switch it's dark.
I can (*) blow a candle out,
(At * give a generous puff)
And then snuff out the spark!
I can (*) put the campfire out,
(At * mime pouring water)
For water kills the flames that danced and swirled.
But you can't turn off, no, you can't put out,
No, you can't quench the light of the world.

They once turned the light off
When they hung him up to die.
They thought it would kill him
When they called out 'Crucify!'
He laid down his life for us
As God's great plan unfurled…
But you can't turn off, no, you can't put out,
No, you can't quench the light of the world.

He rose and his light shines
And gives life to all who choose to follow him.
He brings hope to darkness
And his love will never dim.
He can set our hearts on fire,
And guide us when our lives seem black as night.
For you can't turn off, no, you can't put out,
No, you can't quench the world's source of light.

TEASPOON PRAYER

Thanks: Thank you that you were prepared to give up your life for us on the cross so that you could bring light into our darkness.

Sorry: We are sorry that we sometimes prefer our own darkness to your light.

Please: Please help others to see your light shining in us.

No one can switch off the light of the world

I can (*) switch the light off!

(At * make the sound of the light switch by clicking fingers)

With the flick of a switch it's dark.

I can (*) blow a candle out,

(At * give a generous puff)

And then snuff out the spark!

I can (*) put the campfire out,

(At * mime pouring water)

For water kills the flames that danced and swirled.

But you can't turn off, no, you can't put out,

No, you can't quench the light of the world.

They once turned the light off

When they hung him up to die.

They thought it would kill him

When they called out 'Crucify!'

He laid down his life for us

As God's great plan unfurled...

But you can't turn off, no, you can't put out,

No, you can't quench the light of the world.

He rose and his light shines

And gives life to all who choose to follow him.

He brings hope to darkness

And his love will never dim.

He can set our hearts on fire,

And guide us when our lives seem black as night.

For you can't turn off, no, you can't put out,

No, you can't quench the world's source of light.

Reproduced with permission from *Does Jesus Like Cake?* published by BRF 2003 (1 84101 319 6)

Chapter 9

SAYING SORRY

> *Don't get so angry that you sin. Don't go to bed angry.*
>
> EPHESIANS 4:26

'Why is it that everyone always has the latest stuff except me?' thought Robby, dragging his shoes as he walked past a shop window full of computers, mobile phones and cameras. 'I think I must be the only one in my class who doesn't have a mobile, and there's definitely no one else who's only allowed to play on the computer at the weekend.'

That suddenly reminded him. Today was Friday. That meant he might be allowed to play a little on the computer in the evening. A friend had lent him a new computer game at school and Robby could hardly wait to try it out. He quickened his pace.

On the way home, he considered the best way to go about things. If only Jim were there, there wouldn't be a problem. It was Mum who was so difficult about the computer. All his friends' mums let them play on the computer whenever they felt like it. His mother made up stupid rules like 'only at the weekend', and 'only after home-work and violin practice'. He considered. He could say it was part of his homework and just quickly jump into Word if he heard her outside the door.

But when Robby reached home, there was a surprise awaiting him. He couldn't use the computer because there was someone else using it, and that person was Mum. Robby just couldn't believe it—Mum at the computer! Why, she didn't even know how to switch it on.

'What are you doing, Mum?' he asked, slinging his bag down on to the floor and letting his coat droop down on top of it. Instead of answering him, Mum shouted for his dad.

'Paul, could you come here a sec? I pressed "send" and now my letter has disappeared. I can't see it anywhere. Oh no, I think it's lost because I didn't save it—and it took me a whole hour to write it.' Her voice ended on a wail.

'I've shown you that three times already!' came Dad's voice from the bathroom. 'It hasn't disappeared. It's just gone into the "out" box.'

Mum fiddled wildly with the keyboard.

'Oh no! Now it's gone all black!' she shrieked. 'Please hurry up!'

From the bathroom came a loud sigh. There was the sound of the toilet flushing and the tap going on, then Dad emerged.

'Look, all you have to do is press "send", then "send and receive",' he began, and then stopped. 'What on earth are you doing now?' he asked, and his voice was of the kind that made Robby softly slink away into the kitchen where he shut the door so that he couldn't hear them. He got himself a cup of milk and raided the biscuit tins.

Why was Mum suddenly into the computer? She had once, long ago, tried to learn how to use it, but had given up because she found it so frustrating. The voices, though muffled by the kitchen door, got louder. Robby took a catalogue that was lying on the kitchen table and started to flick through it. He found the sports section and began to study the training shoes. Wow! Andrew Tolhurst had some just like those black ones. Fifty pounds! Robby knew he would never own such expensive trainers.

'It's just not fair!' he thought, looking down at his own uncool feet, clad in a pair of new trainers which had been on offer at the supermarket. They were bright red. He had already been teased about them at school. He turned to the toys section. Hey, mega cool! There was Steve Flowers' remote control jeep! He had bought that with his own pocket money he'd told Robby. Robby looked at the price. How had Steven managed to save up all that?

'He must get about three times as much as me,' thought Robby gloomily. 'And I bet his dad never forgets to give it to him, like mine does'.

Through the closed kitchen door, Mum and Dad were still at it.

'I just don't believe this!' He could hear Mum's voice. 'Why can't you show me slowly? Is it so difficult for you to appreciate that different people think in different ways? What is the difference between a folder and a document, anyway? There's no need to make that face, you know. I can't help it. I just don't understand. But you're just making me feel even more stupid than I do already.'

'Calm down!' shouted Dad's voice crossly. 'Now, to get the disk out, you just press that knob there… No, not that one! Oh, for heaven's sake! You've turned the whole thing off now! Now you've probably lost everything.'

A door slammed loudly, then there was silence. Robby opened the kitchen door and peeked out. Quietly he walked to the front door and looked into the study. Dad was staring at the computer screen and pressing various keys. He had his 'do not disturb' face on. Mum was

nowhere to be seen. Robby slipped out of the front door and sat down on the stairs. He was thinking hard.

'If I had those new trainers now, they wouldn't help Mum and Dad stop quarrelling,' he thought. 'And if I had my own mobile, that wouldn't be much use either.'

Slowly and aimlessly, he made his way downstairs to Jim's flat and knocked. Jim was in the kitchen doing his ironing. Next to him, in a plastic washing basket, lay a mountain of white shirts, chef's hats, countless tea towels and some tablecloths.

'Hello, Robby,' said Jim. 'What's up?'

Robby sighed. 'Can I watch you iron for a bit?' he asked.

'Certainly,' said Jim. His brow was glistening with little beads of perspiration as he attacked the creases in a shirt.

'Do you like ironing, Jim?' asked Robby.

'No, not much,' replied Jim. 'But there is something quite satisfying in turning this…' (and he held up the crumpled shirt) '… into that.' He pointed to a neat row of freshly ironed shirts hanging in his open closet.

'Ironing is just part of the rough-and-tumble of life,' he continued. 'First the clothes are all lovely and clean and fresh. Then you wear them. The clothes get dirty, then they have to be washed.

Then the creases have to be ironed out. Then you put them on and they get dirty again. And they need to be washed. Then ironed again. It never stops. You're never finished.'

He paused. From upstairs, Mum and Dad's voices floated down, muffled but still obviously cross. Hasty footsteps moved resolutely over Jim's ceiling. Jim glanced at Robby.

'Sounds as though there are some creases that need ironing out upstairs!' said Jim, with a grin. 'Don't you worry,' he added, seeing Robby's face. 'Quarrels are part of the rough-and-tumble of life, too. But your mum and dad know how to deal with that. Relationships are like T-shirts. They are constantly getting dirty, needing a wash and then needing the creases smoothed out.'

Robby pondered. Was that all that was going on upstairs? Just smoothing out crumples?

'But how do you get rid of the creases in relationships?' asked Robby.

'Well, in the long run,' said Jim, 'the best way to get rid of those creases is to smooth them out with that little tiny word, "sorry". It works wonders, you know. "Sorry" may look small, like this iron, but it's immensely powerful.' Jim pressed a button on his iron and a jet of steam shot out with a business-like hiss.

Suddenly, Robby heard the sound of his own front door being opened upstairs. He darted out of Jim's flat and saw Mum coming down the stairs. She was carrying a little bag, and even from downstairs, Robby could see that her eyes looked all red. Suddenly he felt a stab of fear. He rushed upstairs two at a time and flung his arms round Mum, burying his face in her coat.

'Where are you going, Mum?' he mumbled.

'Hello, Robby. Where's your school bag? Have you just come home?'

'No, I've been home for ages. I don't think you saw me. I've been hearing you and Dad… Don't go away, Mum.'

His mother hugged him.

'Mum, what are you doing?'

She looked down at his serious face.

'Just now I'm very angry with Dad,' she said, 'because he can't show me things on the computer in a way that I can understand. But I'm even more angry with the stupid computer—and with the Music Director at work, who is insisting that we communicate by e-mail. But most of all, I'm angry with myself for being too old-fashioned, too stupid, to grasp what every child can do with no trouble at all on the computer nowadays.'

'Where are you going, Mum?' asked Robby.

'Well, I thought, rather than go on shouting at Dad, I'd just go out for a little walk. But on second thoughts, I think I'll go in again and have a nice cup of coffee with you and with Dad. And the others—Anna and Andy will be home soon.'

She pushed open the door and they went in. Dad was still clicking away on the computer. Mum went over to him and draped her arms round him.

'Sorry I'm such a useless pupil,' she said. Dad looked surprised. He was silent for a minute, rubbing his forehead until it went all red. Then at last he answered.

'Sorry I'm such a rubbish teacher,' he said slowly. 'I've had an idea,' he continued. 'Why don't we ask Janet if she can show you a thing or two on the computer?'

Mum wrinkled her nose thoughtfully. Janet was a good friend of hers.

'I don't think I want Janet to see how stupid I am,' she said. 'And I can't shout at her when I get cross.'

'That's the point,' said Dad.

'I'll think about it,' promised Mum. 'Did you send the e-mail?'

'Yes,' said Dad.

'Good. Let's go and have some cake to celebrate.'

Soon Robby was happily kicking his untrendy red trainers under the table while he consumed a large slice of succulent, homemade chocolate cake, with Dad munching away on one side of him and Mum on the other. So what if he didn't get as much pocket money as the others in his class? There were some things that money just couldn't buy.

Squidgy squodgy squares

Here is a recipe for the very delicious cake that Robby has just enjoyed.

★ 100g plain chocolate
★ 250g butter
★ 4 eggs
★ 350g sugar
★ 100g plain flour
★ 2 teaspoons baking powder
★ 225g ground almonds
   (optional—can be replaced
   with 100g plain flour)

1. Melt together butter and chocolate in a roomy saucepan.

2. When melted, allow to cool a little, then add all dry ingredients.

3. Add the four eggs, mixing thoroughly.

4. Scrape mixture into a greased and floured baking tray tin (approximately 40cm by 30cm with a rim at least 2cm high)

5. Bake at 180°C for 30 minutes and take out while mixture still looks squidgy.

6. Leave in the tin to harden for about 10 minutes before cutting into squares.

Reproduced with permission from *Does Jesus Like Cake?* published by BRF 2003 (1 84101 319 6)

TINY BUT POWERFUL—ALL ABOUT THE WORD 'SORRY'

Do you ever feel, like Robby, that everyone else has the latest stuff except you? Robby made the discovery that some very valuable things in life are worth far more than trendy clothes or the latest electronic equipment, but that these things are absolutely free. One of these very valuable things is that little word 'sorry'. Saying sorry doesn't cost any money at all but sometimes it costs us an awful lot of courage, whether we are adults or children. Of course, quarrels and arguments do happen—that's part of life. God's recipe book, the Bible, has a good recipe to use when we get angry and annoyed with other people.

Ephesians 4:26 says, 'Don't get so angry that you sin. Don't go to bed angry.' It's a good rule not to let your anger outlive the day but to try to make up before you go to sleep. Mostly, it's true to say that it takes two to make a quarrel, so both people need to say sorry and to forgive. 'Sorry' is such a tiny little word, but appearances are deceptive: it is also immensely powerful! It can defuse dangerous situations, which are threatening to get out of control.

Saying sorry can be very difficult. It can also be hard when someone says sorry to you. How do you react? Sometimes you can feel so angry that you simply want to punch the other person on the nose! Do you think that would be a good idea? Guess what? We often deserve a punch on the nose ourselves! We all often need to say sorry to God and to ask for his forgiveness. And he always does forgive us. So it's a good idea if we remember that although we are not perfect ourselves, God forgives us. Therefore we can afford to be generous to others when they say sorry to us. Being both forgiven and able to forgive is so important that Jesus included it in the model prayer that he gave us—the Lord's Prayer.

Father, help us to honour your name. Come and set up your kingdom. Give us each day the food we need. Forgive us our sins, as we forgive everyone who has done wrong to us. And keep us from being tempted.

LUKE 11:2–4

When you have a quarrel in your family, do you have a habit of saying sorry to each other, or do you just go off in a huff and leave it at that? Or are you the type of person who likes an argument to fester—to drag on, get more serious, continue for a week without speaking to the other person? The recipe in Ephesians is a good one, because it stops arguments from turning bitter and getting more serious and eventually doing a lot of harm. It's funny, but if we go on being convinced we are right and the other person is a stupid twit and completely wrong, eventually that does more harm than good to us. The person who is unable to say sorry suffers the most in the long run.

A SONG TO SING

S. O. R. R. Y. Sorry can be hard to say.
But once it's heard,
That little tiny word
Can clear a lot of trouble away.
It may take grit
To come out with it
But sorry really makes your day…
Sorry, sorry, sorry, as the sun goes down,
Let me try a smile and wipe off the frown.
Sorry, sorry, sorry, let's forget our fight
And live our lives as children of the light.

TEASPOON PRAYER

Thanks: Thank you, Lord Jesus, that we can iron out the creases and crumples in our relationships with the little word 'sorry'.

Sorry: I want to think about anything I may need to say sorry about.

Please: If I need to go and say sorry to a person, please help me to have the courage to do so.

Sorry

S. O. R. R. Y. Sorry can be hard to say.

But once it's heard,

That little tiny word

Can clear a lot of trouble away.

It may take grit

To come out with it

But sorry really makes your day…

Sorry, sorry, sorry, as the sun goes down,

Let me try a smile and wipe off the frown.

Sorry, sorry, sorry, let's forget our fight

And live our lives as children of the light.

Chapter 10

PUMPKINS AND PRICKLES

(A HARVEST STORY)

Jesus said to his disciples: 'I am the true vine, and my Father is the gardener. He cuts away every branch of mine that doesn't produce fruit. But he trims clean every branch that does produce fruit, so that it will produce even more fruit...

Stay joined to me, and I will stay joined to you. Just as a branch cannot produce fruit unless it stays joined to the vine, you cannot produce fruit unless you stay joined to me. I am the vine, and you are the branches. If you stay joined to me, and I stay joined to you, then you will produce lots of fruit. But you cannot do anything without me.'

JOHN 15:1–2, 4–5

In these verses from John's Gospel, Jesus was drawing a picture. But he wasn't using brushes and paints—he was using words. He was painting a picture of a mighty vine with its branches groaning beneath the weight of the luscious clusters of fruit growing on it. Do you know what kind of fruit a vine produces? Have you ever tried to grow anything? When Anna tried to grow something, she discovered that the kind of fruit you find in a fruit bowl is not the only kind there is!

The old apple tree in Anna's garden had so many apples that Mum didn't know what to do with them all. But Jim was in his element. He made countless apple pies, apple strudels, and apple-fudge crumbles, and froze them all ready for the harvest supper at church. Anna was busy planning for harvest too. They were going to have a harvest assembly at her school.

'It would be a very nice idea,' Miss Parkinson, Anna's teacher, had said, 'if all of you could try to bring something for our harvest assembly this year. Our class is responsible for decorating the hall. Maybe some of you with gardens could even grow something yourselves.'

Anna was inspired. She begged Mum for her own piece of garden. It was very small, just a narrow strip at the end of the vegetable plot. With her pocket money she bought a packet of broccoli seeds, her favourite vegetable. Mum showed her how to make straight lines in the earth and then place the seeds in them and carefully cover them with soil. 'But Anna, this garden is your responsibility,' she said. 'Don't expect me to weed or water it for you. I've got enough to do.'

Anna nodded happily. This was going to be the best garden in the whole world! The first day, she watered it five times; the second day, twice. The third day she remembered in the evening, and the fourth day she went to Gina Evan's birthday party and forgot altogether. Then the children went to stay with Granny for a week.

When she came back from Granny's, Anna ran out to have a look at her garden. There she discovered Jim, sitting in a stripy deckchair that was threatening to split beneath the weight of his large behind. Scattered around him in the grass were jam jars of water, pencils, brushes and a paintbox. Anna peeped over his shoulder and gasped at his vibrant, colourful painting. It was a picture of the apple tree, bending beneath its many rosy clusters of fruit.

'That's beautiful, Jim!' said Anna.

Jim studied the picture, his head on one side. 'I want to be like that apple tree,' he said.

Anna laughed. She wasn't quite sure what he meant, but in his rather grubby T-shirt, balancing a pad on the wobbly ledge that his tummy made when he sat down, he didn't remind her of an apple tree at all.

'What do you mean?' she asked.

'I want to produce lots of fine fruit,' he said, adding a few more apples to the tree with his paintbrush.

'You mean you want to be a gardener?' asked Anna.

He smiled.

'No, I'm quite happy cooking the things gardeners produce. But all of us are a bit like this apple tree. Every time we do or say something, we are producing fruit. Sometimes what comes out is like that…' and he pointed at a brown, squidgy apple that was rotting in the grass near his foot. 'That's when we only think of ourselves and don't care if we hurt other people. But if we want to live our lives with Jesus, then he will help us to show love to other people, so that the things we say and do are like a crop of delicious fruit.'

Anna picked up a windfall from the ground and bit into its juicy sweetness as she went to look at her little garden. There she found a fine, delicate fuzz of green in a nice straight row. She watered the seedlings and then went back inside.

During the next two weeks, it rained solidly and Anna forgot all about her garden. The snails and slugs didn't, though. They munched and crunched and thoroughly enjoyed themselves.

A week before the harvest assembly, Anna's teacher reminded the children about harvest and asked them what they were going to bring.

'I've grown a pumpkin as big as this,' said James Hampton, holding out his hands.

'I've got some carrots,' called out Fiona Barrett.

'I'm growing some cress,' said Janita Sharma.

'I've got some broccoli,' said Anna proudly. 'I grew it all by myself!' she added.

'I hate broccoli,' said James. 'I'm allergic to it. It makes me sick.'

On Wednesday, Anna got up early and went out to her garden with some sharp scissors. She snipped through the rather wiggly row of green stalks.

'That's funny,' she thought to herself. 'I thought broccoli was supposed to have green flower things. The ones on here seem to be very small. Maybe you can eat the leaves as well, like cabbage. Ow! It's quite prickly!'

She picked a bowlful, slid the stalks into a plastic bag and went indoors to eat her breakfast. Dad came down in his pyjamas to supervise the packed lunches.

'Look at my broccoli, Dad!' said Anna.

'Lovely,' he said absently, taking his first swig of coffee.

Fifteen minutes later, Anna set off, jauntily swinging her carrier bag. The nearer she got to school, the more children appeared, laden down with vegetables of all shapes and sizes.

Miss Parkinson was already in the assembly hall, helping the children from Anna's class to arrange all the fruit and vegetables on the stage. She was obviously in one of her bad moods,

snapping sharply as an apple rolled off the windowsill on to the floor. Almost all the class were there already, busily decorating the ledges with apples and flowers. James Hampton was just presenting Miss Parkinson with a huge orange pumpkin. Anna went towards them.

'Look at my pumpkin, Anna!' shouted James. 'What've you got?'

Anna opened her plastic bag.

'I've got some broccoli and I grew it myself,' she said. Everyone crowded round to peer inside the bag.

'That's not broccoli!' said James loudly. 'Those are thistles.' There was a moment's silence, and then everyone began to laugh.

'Anna's brought a whole bag of thistles!' shrieked someone.

'They aren't thistles!' said Anna indignantly. 'Look, Miss Parkinson. These aren't thistles, are they?'

'Come along, we haven't got all day!' snapped Miss Parkinson, grabbing the bag from Anna and peering into it crossly.

'They look just like thistles to me,' she said shortly and handed the bag back to Anna.

'But I planted them!' said Anna. 'I've been watering them and weeding them.'

'You pulled out the seeds and left all the weeds!' shouted James. 'Oh wow! That rhymes! I'm a poet

and I didn't know it!' He considered for a few minutes, his head on one side. Then he began to sing to the tune of 'Mary, Mary quite contrary'.

'Anna, Anna's quite bananas,
How does her garden grow?
With lots of seeds that turn out weeds,
And thistles all in a row, row, row,
And thistles all in a row.'

Anna just couldn't believe it. She stared into her bag. She concentrated hard on swallowing the big lump that she could feel in her throat. James was belting out his song and leaping around, the others joining in.

'To think that I spent all that time watering thistles,' she said to herself. Her face tried out a tiny smile.

'Do you like my poem, Anna?' asked James, surprised.

'Yes, I do. It's very good,' said Anna. 'But Anna and banana don't quite rhyme, you know.'

'They do if you sing it with an American accent,' yelled James triumphantly, and did so. To his annoyance, Anna joined in loudly. As she did so, she noticed something on James' pumpkin.

'Did you grow that pumpkin yourself?' she asked.

James nodded.

'Then why has it got a label on it saying two pounds fifty?' she asked sweetly. The bell rang for assembly and the other classes began to pour into the hall. There was no time for James to give an answer. He just stuck out his tongue. Anna sat down in her place, still clutching the plastic bag tightly in her hot hands. Miss Parkinson came up on to the stage.

'Good morning, children,' she said.

'Good morning, Miss Parkinson. Good morning, everybody,' chorused Dingway Primary School. As she joined in, Anna had a sudden idea. Quickly she slid a thistle along the row of chairs on to James' place—just in time.

'Please sit down,' said Miss Parkinson, and everybody did. Everybody except James. He jumped up again quickly with a piercing squeal. Miss Parkinson glared at him. He removed the thistle gingerly and sat down again.

'James, stay behind after assembly today, please,' she said icily. James' face went bright red and he stared at the ground as the piano began to thump out 'We plough the fields and scatter'. Anna didn't sing. She stared into her bag of thistles. Although James had deserved it, she still felt sorry. Miss Narky Parky was a force to be reckoned with when she got angry.

'She can be as spiky as my thistles,' thought Anna. She looked round at all the fruit and vegetables arranged up on the stage. Suddenly she remembered what Jim had said about wanting to be like the apple tree, producing fine fruit. Now, not only had she grown a whole load of thistles, but she had used them to get James into a very prickly situation!

After assembly, everyone filed out—everyone except James. At the door, Anna turned and saw him standing against the wall looking very uncomfortable.

'I'll do it! Please help me, Lord Jesus!' she muttered, and ran into the assembly hall again, straight towards Miss Parkinson.

'Miss Parkinson! I'm sorry, it was my fault that James jumped up like that. You see, I thought these thistles were broccoli, and when they weren't, I just put one on his chair and it pricked him when he sat down.' She stopped, panting for breath. James came over looking very surprised.

'What have you got to say for yourself, James?' asked Miss Parkinson.

'I teased her. So it was my fault too,' he said. There was a short pause. Then he added, 'And I didn't really grow that pumpkin. Mum bought it for me. I planted loads of pumpkin seeds, but they didn't come up.'

Miss Parkinson took off her glasses and polished them.

'Well, if this is confession time, I may as well join in,' she said. 'I was all in a fluster about the assembly today, and maybe just a tad hasty. Why don't we all shake hands and get everything packed into these shoeboxes. We've got a busy day ahead of us, taking all these goodies round to people who need them. They love the fruit and vegetables. But most of all, I think they love the children's visits.'

All three of them shook hands and Anna gave a little jump. She couldn't wait to get home and tell Jim about it all.

Chocolate fruit

★ Different types of fruit pieces (for example, grapes, sliced bananas, strawberries, sliced apples)
★ Small bowls of freshly melted and still-warm brown or white cake-topping chocolate
★ Large circles of baking parchment on plates
★ Cocktail sticks

Chocolate fruit looks very inviting. You might want to provide little bags so that the children can take some home. However, tell them that they need to keep it in the fridge, and should eat it within two days.

Make sure you have enough fruit pieces for the size of your group, and enough bowls of chocolate to allow no more than four children to a bowl. You will need as many plates as you have bowls.

1. Use the cocktail sticks to spear pieces of fruit and dip them into the chocolate mixture.

2. Lay the fruit on the baking parchment, and place in the fridge until the chocolate has set.

FRUITFUL LIVES

You need:
★ A picture of a vine bearing lots of fruit
★ A branch broken off a tree (the deader the better)

Questions

• What do you think Anna wanted to tell Jim about?

• In the end, Anna did produce some good fruit for the harvest assembly. What do you think it was?

• Sometimes the things we or other people do and say can be rather 'thistly'. Can you think of any examples? (Maybe the group leader could have a few personal 'thistle experiences' ready to share.)

Jim painted a beautiful picture of a tree. Jesus also once painted a picture of a tree—only he didn't use colours, he used words. His picture was of something that his disciples would have known as well as we know apple trees—a vine. Have any of you ever seen a vine? *(Show them your picture.)*

Jesus said that living our lives with him is rather like being a branch on a vine. In the Bible he says:

'I am the true vine, and my Father is the gardener. He cuts away every branch of mine that doesn't produce fruit. But he trims clean every branch that does produce fruit, so that it will produce even more fruit...

Stay joined to me, and I will stay joined to you. Just as a branch cannot produce fruit unless it stays joined to the vine, you cannot produce fruit unless you stay joined to me. I am the vine, and you are the branches. If you stay joined to me, and I stay joined to you, then you will produce lots of fruit. But you cannot do anything without me.'

JOHN 15:1–2, 4–5

(Hold up a branch.) Now here's a nice branch. I broke it off my apple tree. I thought I would put it in my bedroom so that I don't have to go outside to pick the apples. I'll be able to just pick them from my bed. Do you think it will produce many apples next autumn? You don't think it will? Oh! Why not?

Of course, once you break a branch away from the main trunk, it dies. Why is that? What does the trunk of a tree do for its branches? By drawing up water from the ground, it provides the branches with the life-giving sap, which enables it to produce leaves and fruit.

Jesus compared himself with the stem of a vine, and said that his special friends, his

disciples, were like the branches. Jesus knew that he was about to be taken prisoner, and he knew that his disciples would feel completely lost and confused and very sad when that happened. That was why, shortly before he was taken away by the soldiers, he painted this word-picture for them. He did it to show them that he would be there even if they couldn't see him, that if they clung to the truths he had told them, like branches joined on to a vine, then they would be able to draw from him all that they needed to stay alive and produce fruit.

Christians believe that all this counts for us too. If we want to be Jesus' special friends and decide that we want to live our lives with him, then it is as though we become attached, joined up to him, like branches attached to a tree. That means that his love can flow through us and that enables us to 'be fruitful'. What kind of fruit does Jesus want us to produce?

A SONG TO SING

We
Are just like branches on a tree,
Drawing strength and energy
From the trunk that holds us ready, steady,
To bring forth juicy fruities!
He
Is always there for you and me
If we cling on happily
To the life-giving tree.
Oh, oh, oh,
Jesus is the vine
And the branches that entwine
Are fed with love,
That comes from heav'n above!
And the grapes are really great,
For they have no sell-by date,
For love is made
To neither rot nor fade.

TEASPOON PRAYER

Thanks: Thank you, Lord Jesus, for all the harvest gifts. Thank you as well that in our lives we also bring forth a harvest. Please help it to be a good one. You love us so much and we know that you are always with us, supporting us as the stem of a tree supports its branches.

Sorry: Sorry when we forget that you are there or try to do things our own way.

Please: Please help us to love one another.

A GAME TO PLAY

Fruit salad

We've been talking about producing fruit. Now we're going to play a very fruity game!

Sitting in a circle, the group leader gets every child to choose the name of a fruit and say it out loud. When every-body has chosen one, go round the circle again to make sure everyone still knows what he or she is.

One child, seated in the middle, is the guesser.

The group leader starts by calling out somebody else's fruit—for example, 'pineapple'.

Whoever is 'pineapple' has to quickly call out the fruit name of another player—let's say 'strawberry'. If the guesser in the middle correctly identifies the player with the name 'strawberry' by pointing at him or her before 'strawberry' has got round to shouting out the next fruit, then 'strawberry' has to go into the middle and become the next guesser.

If a player accidentally calls out the fruit name of the person in the middle, then that player has to go into the middle and become the guesser.

The Grapevine Song

We
Are just like branches on a tree,
Drawing strength and energy
From the trunk that holds us ready, steady,
To bring forth juicy fruities!
He
Is always there for you and me
If we cling on happily
To the life-giving tree.
Oh, oh, oh, Jesus is the vine
And the branches that entwine
Are fed with love,
That comes from heav'n above!
And the grapes are really great,
For they have no sell-by date,
For love is made
To neither rot nor fade.

Chapter 11

FRIENDS

> *And religion does make your life rich, by making you content with what you have. We didn't bring anything into this world, and we won't take anything with us when we leave.*
>
> 1 TIMOTHY 6:6–7

I wonder if you have ever been to a friend's house and come back home thinking: 'Wow! So-and-so is so lucky! I wish I had…' and there follows a whole list of possibilities (or impossibilities) ranging from a Barbie doll to a Gameboy to a swimming pool to curly hair to more pocket money.

Here is what happened to Andy and Robby when they went to visit some friends.

Alex was bouncing on the sofa. 'Come on!' he shouted to Andy. 'Try it! It's really bouncy!'

Andy glanced over at Alex's mother, who was reading on the sheepskin rug in front of the open fire that was crackling in the grate.

'Doesn't your mum mind if we bounce on the sofa?' he asked timidly. He knew that his mum would go berserk if he and a friend started treating the couch like a trampoline. Alex's mum rolled over and smiled.

'What a well brought-up little boy you are!' she said. 'But that sofa is really ancient and incredibly ugly. I can hardly wait until it breaks, and Alex is certainly doing his best to help it meet its doom soon. So you're welcome to have a bounce. But don't think that means you can bounce on the one in the sitting-room.'

'I thought this was the sitting-room,' said Andy, bewildered. He had never been to his school-friend Alex's house before, and it was huge.

'No, this is the snug—that's what we call our family room,' replied his mother. 'Alex, haven't you shown Andy the house yet? Go and show him the rest.'

Obediently Alex bounced off the sofa, and Andy followed him out of the snug and into the wide entrance hall. There was a door leading off at the other end and Alex gave it a push. It swung open to reveal a large room, which was dominated by a long, dark wooden table with at least twelve matching chairs around it.

'That's the dining-room,' said Alex casually.

'You must have a big family,' said Andy. He had thought Alex only had two elder sisters.

'Oh, we hardly ever eat in there. It's just for when Mum and Dad have guests,' said Alex. 'We always eat in the kitchen.' He pushed open the next door. 'And that's the sitting-room.'

A majestic grandfather clock ticked away solemnly in the corner, behind a polished grand piano, which was surrounded by armchairs, sofas and little polished tables.

'Actually, that sofa over there is really great for bouncing on,' said Alex with a grin. 'Shall we have a quick go?'

'No,' said Andy. 'Show me your room.'

Alex made for the wide stairs. Andy eyed the banisters. They looked great for sliding down.

Alex's room was big and very messy. His bookshelf was overflowing on to the floor and there were odd socks everywhere. In the corner stood a rickety-looking table-tennis table and on it, surrounded by half-broken Lego models, was enthroned a computer. Andy felt at home at once.

'What shall we play first?' he asked.

Meanwhile, Andy's brother Robby was visiting Jasmin, his friend from school. It was the first time he had ever been to Jasmin's house and he was a little nervous. Jasmin's mum was very welcoming.

'Hello, Robby, how nice to see you. Jasmin is so pleased that you could come. Now, you must both be hungry. What would you like to eat?'

'Make us some hot chocolate,' pleaded Jasmin. Her mother smiled and started clinking around in the kitchen. Robby was relieved. He had been a little worried about the food side of things. Jasmin often had snacks at school that looked quite different from the kind of food Robby's family ate. Robby knew how to make hot chocolate himself. You just poured the milk in the mug, put it in the microwave for a minute and then stirred in two spoons of chocolate powder (three, when Mum wasn't looking). But in Jasmin's family, it seemed a more lengthy procedure. Her mum was grating chocolate from a large bar, and heating up the milk in a little pan. When it was warm, she added the chocolate and then used a little gadget to whisk up the milk until it was foaming. She poured it into two cups and then squirted some whipped cream on top. This she decorated with some more of the grated chocolate and then handed it to the children. Gingerly, Robby took a sip. Rich, creamy, sweet delight flowed into his mouth.

'That's the best hot chocolate I've ever tasted!' he exclaimed. Jasmin's mother looked pleased.

'Try one of these,' she said, passing over a plate of golden, squiggly, spiral-like things. Robby's

heart sank. Even as he was considering how he could politely refuse, Jasmin reached out, broke off a piece and thrust it to Robby's lips.

'Just taste!' she commanded.

Unwillingly, Robby opened his mouth. The thing was soaked in a sweet syrup, yet at the same time as being gooey with syrup it was crispy and crunchy inside. Robby was enchanted. He ate another six.

Afterwards, they went up to Jasmin's room. She was lucky, thought Robby enviously. She had a room to herself, and she had her own TV.

They watched a bit of TV and then designed a poster for their science project. Robby had a wonderful afternoon, until suddenly it was time for supper. And he needn't have worried about that either. They had the most delicious chicken he had ever eaten in his life.

That evening, Alex's mum brought Andy home on her way to a party. Andy waved goodbye and then ran up the steps and pushed open the front door. He stood and stared. Why had he never noticed before how narrow the steps were that led from the front door up to their flat? And the hall looked so dark and dingy. Slowly he plodded up the stairs and opened the door at the top. He dumped his bag on the floor and went into the sitting-room. Mum, already wrapped up in her

shabby old dressing-gown, was lying on the sofa, reading the newspaper.

'Oh, hello!' she greeted him. 'You gave me a fright!' She jumped up to give him a welcome-home hug, but he slipped out of her embrace and went over to the room he shared with Robby. He flung open the door and regarded it gloomily. It was so small! And Robby's Lego was all over his side of the room. Everything here was unbearable. How had he managed to put up with it so long?

Robby, also back from his visit, was lying on his bed, gazing at the ceiling.

'Hello, Andy,' he said with a yawn. 'How was it at Alex's?'

'It was just fantastic,' answered Andy. 'He lives in the most amazing house, and they've got a huge garden and his mum lets him bounce on the sofa and watch TV much later than we're allowed to. And he's got his own room and his own computer.'

'So has Jasmin,' said Robby with a sigh. 'And her mum cooks delicious food and she's so nice, too. She smiles all the time.'

'This just seems like such a dump, now,' said Andy and flung himself down on his bed.

Just then Mum came in.

'I've got a surprise for you,' she said in an excited kind of voice. 'I've been given five complimentary tickets for *Aladdin*, the pantomime I'm playing in next week. I thought you two could ask Jasmin and Alex along. We could have pizza here first, and then all drive over to the theatre.'

'Oh no, Mum,' cried Andy. 'Don't ask Alex!'

'Why not?' she asked. 'Didn't you get on well with him today?'

'Yes, of course I did—very well,' said Andy. 'But...' he paused, struggling for words.

'I'm really sorry,' said Mum, 'but his mum rang me around tea-time. She told me how well you two boys were getting on and how lonely Alex sometimes gets on his own, because his two big sisters are much older than him—they're already grown up. Anyway, I was so sure that both you and he would be delighted that I've already invited him.'

Andy writhed on his bed in horror. Alex going with them to a silly, childish pantomime with his mum playing the cello in the orchestra and, worse still, coming for a pizza in their shabby little doll's house of a home?

'Have you ever been to his house, Mum?' he asked.

'No, why?'

'When he sees how we live, he won't want to be friends with me,' he murmured.

Robby saw the look on Mum's face and quickly swallowed what he had been going to say. But he didn't really want Jasmin to come either. It would be awfully embarrassing to go to a pantomime with your own mum playing the cello in the orchestra. Why hadn't Mum learnt a decent instrument, like the electric guitar?

＊

It was a week later. Andy, Alex, Robby, Jasmin and Anna followed the chattering, laughing audience out into the foyer of the theatre. They felt weak with laughter. It had been a fantastic, exhilarating, hilarious and exciting performance, complete with amazing light effects and cool music.

'How did they make the genie disappear like that at the end?' said Jasmin. 'The whole thing was so clever.'

'Wow, Andy,' said Alex, wiping his hot forehead. 'Thanks so much for inviting me. That's one of the best plays I've ever seen. It was just so funny.' And he burst into another chuckle. 'And your mum's cello was out of this world. I never heard a cello doing jazz before. What a shame it's over. Do you think I could come to your house again some time? Maybe I could even stay the night.'

Special drinking chocolate

* Four chunks good-quality chocolate per person
* 1 cup milk per person
* Either a blob of whipped cream flavoured with a little sugar and vanilla essence, or a marshmallow to decorate

Each child can grate his or her own chocolate with a cheese grater. (Or use a food processor if you want less mess.)

1. Warm the milk until it is almost boiling.

2. Add the grated chocolate to the milk, stir until the chocolate has melted, then froth it up with a milk frother or a whisk.

3. Decorate with a blob of whipped cream or a marshmallow.

Sit in a circle, perhaps light a few candles, hold warm mugs in cupped hands, take tiny sips and enjoy!

Reproduced with permission from *Does Jesus Like Cake?* published by BRF 2003 (1 84101 319 6)

CONTENTMENT

You need:
☆ A bowl of fruit (pear, apple, orange, pineapple, banana, melon, strawberry and a bunch of grapes would be ideal)
☆ A bowl with eight bananas
☆ A hand mirror

Today we're going to think about discontentment. When we are discontented we are not happy with the way things are. Sometimes it can be a good thing not to be contented with something. If we get a bad mark for maths and we know we could do better if we worked a little harder, then it's a good idea not to be satisfied with that mark and to try to do better next time. Often, though, we are discontented with things that we are not able to change.

Can you remember what Andy was discontented with in the story?

Did Alex enjoy his return visit to Andy? Do you think he found Andy's house small and scruffy?

Can you think of anything that you have been discontented about?

Here are a few things other children have said.

'I wish I had a nicer nose, like Jane.'

'It's not fair, Tim has all the fun and I'm never allowed to do anything.'

'I wish my mum wasn't so fat. If only she looked a bit more like Lorraine's mum.'

'I can never invite anyone home because I don't want my friends to see how small our house is.'

We can become so concerned about how we will appear to others that we think our homes or families aren't good enough to make the kind of impression we want. Being proud about ourselves makes us dissatisfied with what we have and also makes us feel very worried about what everybody is thinking about us all the time. And that makes us feel very insecure!

The commercials on the television tell us that our lives will be incomplete until we have the product they are advertising. The shops are swarming with people obeying the advertisers'

commands. They lug their new purchases home and immediately all their friends and neighbours are consumed with jealousy until they can afford to get the new thing themselves. Modern life? Or not so modern? Envy and jealousy have always been around—they are as old as the human race. Resenting the fact that others have what you don't have is called 'covetousness' in the Bible, and coveting is something that makes us so miserable that God even included it in his extra special recipe, the Ten Commandments—he told us to nip it in the bud!

Have you ever heard the word 'covet' before? To covet is to wish to have the possessions of

others. It goes beyond just admiring somebody's possessions or thinking, 'I'd like one of those, too.' It leads to envy. Look at this big bowl of fruit. Let's imagine we can hear what each piece of fruit is thinking. Maybe, as we listen, we'll understand a bit more what coveting means. *(Pick up each piece of fruit as it 'talks'. Use the mirror for the pineapple.)*

Imagine the pear says, 'I hate my figure. Pear-shaped hips are so unfashionable. I want to be long and thin. It's not fair. Banana over there has it so good. Look at the way she's flaunting her body.'

And imagine the orange whispers, 'Orange just doesn't suit me. It's not my colour at all. I need something more pale, less obvious. Something a little more like what Banana is wearing. Of course it doesn't suit her at all.'

And imagine the pineapple preening itself in the mirror: 'Tropical, yes. Large and prickly, no. I must do something about this skin. I can't stand Banana. How does she get her skin so smooth?'

And imagine the apple complaining: 'It's not fair. That foreigner, Banana, arrives relaxed and tanned golden after a sea voyage on a luxury cruiser. We Brits just get dumped in the back of a lorry. What a cheek. She cruises, we get bruises.'

And imagine the melon heaving a heavy sigh: 'Life is so unjust. It's too bad to have been landed with such a melancholy name. I wish I could swap with Banana. Some fruits have all the luck.'

And imagine the strawberry's contemptuous snarl: 'Just because Banana's in pyjamas all day, she's made it into the film world. She finds her sleepsuit so 'a-peel-ing'. She thinks it makes her look skinny. Mind you, I wish I had a little more protection. Slugs find me simply irresistible, you know. Flattering, but if Banana would only share a little of her yellow coat with me, their devotion to me wouldn't get so out of control.'

And imagine the grapes' response: 'Gripe, gripe, gripe. It's enough to drive a grape bananas! But Banana is bananas—completely and utterly, there's no doubt about that. She may have a pretty face and an exotic flavour, but ask anyone on the grapevine. She's a banana-brain if ever there was one. We grapes are the pick of the bunch.'

Can you hear how discontented these fruits are? They are so dissatisfied that they are unable to appreciate the good things about themselves. Their main concerns are how they compare with others and what they don't have.

Now just imagine a fairy happens to be flying

around this fruit bowl. She's overheard their conversation and she decides to grant the wishes of the fruit with a wave of her magic wand... Abracadabra! We would end up with this. *(Get rid of the mixed fruit bowl and, with a flourish, produce a bowl of just bananas.)*

Wouldn't it be boring if we all looked the same, all wore the same clothes, all had the same skin colour, and all lived in the same kind of houses? Let's celebrate and enjoy the variety we have in this room, today! Each one of us is completely unique. Each one of us is good at different things. Each one of us looks different. And each one of us has lots of reasons to be content about all sorts of different things. Hooray! As it says in the Bible, being contented is a good recipe for life.

And religion does make your life rich, by making you content with what you have. We didn't bring anything into this world, and we won't take anything with us when we leave.

1 TIMOTHY 6:6–7

SOMETHING TO DO

To celebrate variety, the children could work together to cut up the various fruits. Mix with some natural fruit juice for a delicious, colourful fruit salad full of different textures and flavours. As you chop, talk about the different ways in which the fruit grows, the different countries it comes from, the different shapes of the pips and the stones.

TEASPOON PRAYER

Thank you: Thank you that each one of us has been designed and thought out by God. Thank you for our homes and our families. Thank you that each one of us is special.

Sorry: Sorry that we sometimes fall into the trap of discontentment and feel sorry for ourselves.

Please: Please help us not to compare ourselves with others.

Chapter 12

THE CHRISTMAS PLAY

Don't be jealous or proud, but be humble and consider others more important than your-selves. Care about them as much as you care about yourselves and think the same way that Christ Jesus thought:

Christ was truly God.

But he did not try to remain equal with God.

Instead he gave up everything and became a slave, .

when he became like one of us.

Christ was humble.

He obeyed God and even died on a cross.

PHILIPPIANS 2:3–8

One drizzly, gloomy November day, Robby's teacher, Miss Jones, said to her class: 'You can close your maths books now, because today we are going to start practising for the Christmas play.'

A buzz of excitement greeted her words, desk lids slammed briskly, and very soon class 5a was expressing its hopes and fears for the production very loudly indeed. They were all so busy talking that they didn't notice Miss Jones take out a mini-disk player and position it on the teacher's desk, with the microphone pointing towards the children. Then she held up her hands for silence.

'Please, Miss, what's the play about?' asked Marion Thomson.

'That's a good question, but one which I will answer later,' she said mysteriously. 'I'll just tell you which roles we need first and you can help to decide who plays what. First of all, we need Mary.'

All the girls' hands flew up at once.

'Mary needs to be able to sing well,' she continued, at which a few hands went down again.

'You can't have Jasmin, she's too fat to play Mary!' called out Derek from the back row. There was a general titter, which increased to a roar when Andrew Tolhurst shouted, 'That's all right! The fatter the better! Mary was going to have a baby!'

'Take me, Miss, take me!' pleaded Vandara Sharma. 'I can stuff a cushion up my jumper and look thin again afterwards when the baby's been born. I can sing really well, and I can play "Silent Night" on the recorder.'

'I can sing much better than Vandara,' shrieked Emily Smythe. 'I have singing lessons in London. My mum says I've got a voice like a little angel.'

'An out-of-tune angel!' called out Derek.

Miss Jones stood up, looking at the forest of straining arms.

'Let me tell you some of the other roles before we make a decision,' she said. 'We need a strong lad to play Joseph. Joseph doesn't need to sing a solo, but he does need to plead with all the innkeepers who don't have any room, and they are very rude to him.'

This time the forest of hands all belonged to the boys.

'Don't take Robby, he looks too small!' shouted Kevin Porter.

'And Derek is too fat!' commented Jasmin.

'I've got my black belt in judo!' said Derek, standing up. 'And anyone who says I am fat had better look out. I can bash up any innkeepers who don't want me in their inns. But I don't want old Fatty Jasmin for my wife!'

'We also need some wise men,' continued Miss Jones quietly and went on to list the other roles—shepherds, the angel Gabriel, a choir of angels, and several innkeepers. Robby watched her, puzzled. She didn't usually allow her class to get away with this kind of behaviour. Several boys were in the process of mocking Ben Horner, who wanted to be a wise man, telling him that wise men didn't have tiny brains like his.

A group of girls was busy taking sides about who was the prettiest girl to play Mary, and Miss Jones was watching and listening with a great big grin on her face! Then she turned round and started writing on the board. First of all, she wrote a list of all the roles that they needed. Then her hand moved back up to the name at the top of the list and paused, hovering, above the word 'MARY'. Instantly the noise died down and everybody waited to see what she was going to write.

'Jasmin Softic' she wrote in big letters and proceeded down the list until all the roles were filled. Class 5a's comments were deafening and not very complimentary. Robby lost interest and sneaked the book he was reading out of his school bag. He stuck his fingers in his ears and very soon was away in another world. The next thing he noticed was a big poke in the ribs. Jolted out of his book, he took his fingers out of his ears and found the whole class laughing at him.

'I repeat,' said Miss Jones, 'does anyone not have a role yet?'

Hastily, Robby looked at the board. He couldn't see his name anywhere.

'I don't,' he said.

'Robby,' said his teacher, 'you may be the donkey.'

An outburst of laughter greeted her words.

'Oh yes! Robby is made for that role!' cried out someone. 'Just look at his ears!'

'He'll have to have Jasmin sitting on him! Better do some muscle training, Robby!'

'I always said Robby's a silly ass!'

Suddenly, Miss Jones began to laugh. She laughed and laughed.

'Oh thank you, thank you!' she gasped. 'Class 5a, you were brilliant. You couldn't have been better!'

The class waited in puzzled silence.

Mary – Jasmin   Kings-
Joseph – Frank
Innkeeper – Derek   Shephe
Angel – Vandara
– Emily
– Alice

'You see,' explained Miss Jones, when she had wiped her eyes with a pink pocket handkerchief, 'the nativity play this year is about a class who want to put on a nativity play, just like you. As a matter of fact, you have just helped me to write the scene where the children are given their roles. You see, each child thinks he or she should have one of the star parts. They quarrel so much that two angels who happen to be flying around at that particular moment come down to see what all the noise is about—and this is the kind of thing they hear.'

She picked up her mini-disk player, which was attached to a stereo, and pressed a switch. Loudly and clearly, some familiar voices floated out.

'You can't have Jasmin, she's too fat to play Mary!'

'That's all right! The fatter the better! Mary was going to have a baby!'

'Take me, Miss, take me! I can stuff a cushion up my jumper and look thin again afterwards when the baby's been born. I can sing really well, and I can play "Silent Night" on the recorder.'

'I can sing much better than Vandara. I have singing lessons in London. My mum says I've got a voice like a little angel.'

'An out-of-tune angel!'

'Don't take Robby, he looks too small!'

'And Derek is too fat!'

'I've got my black belt in judo! And anyone who says I am fat had better look out. I can bash up any innkeepers who don't want me in their inns. But I don't want old Fatty Jasmin for my wife!'

Miss Jones clicked off the mini-disk again. Class 5a waited in frozen amazement.

Miss Jones continued, 'Then one of the angels spoke to the other one.

'"Those poor, silly humans!" he said. "They're doing a play about the birth of Jesus, and yet they've completely forgotten about why he came into the world. Look at them all trying to get the best for themselves."

'"Terrible, isn't it?" agreed the other angel. "We'd better do something about it quickly."

'"But what shall we do?" said the first angel.

'"We'll just remind them what it says in the Bible," said the second angel, and he blew on the pages of a Bible that was lying on the table in the classroom. It opened at Philippians 2 verse 3.'

Miss Jones paused and looked at her silent class.

'Would you like to know what it says there?' she asked.

Her class nodded.

'It says that we shouldn't selfishly try to get the best things in life for ourselves, but that we should help one another and look after one another,' she said. 'And the reason we should do this is because of what Jesus was like. Jesus was almighty, all-powerful, but he didn't say "Hey! It's my right to stay in heaven and be equal with God!" Instead, of his own free will, he gave up all his power and allowed himself to be born as a tiny, weak and helpless baby. He was a king, but he didn't try to grab the best palace for himself. Instead he was born in a stable, all mucky and cold.'

Miss Jones paused and looked around the class. 'Do you think it's going to be a good Christmas play?' she asked.

'What happened to those two angels?' asked Robby.

'Hm… I'm not quite sure,' said Miss Jones.

Jasmin put up her hand.

'Please, Miss, I think I know what happened next,' she said. 'One of the girls in that class whose name was Jasmin heard what it says in the Bible, then she put up her hand and said she didn't want to be Mary any more, she just wanted to be a donkey because she felt like one. Then a boy called Derek did the same.' She turned round to look at Derek and he nodded.

'And then Robby said,' she continued, 'that if Jesus humbled himself to become a tiny baby, then, in memory of that, why shouldn't they all become donkeys for the Christmas play and forget about the other roles.'

'Donkeys are actually very useful animals when they are willing to do as they are told. Jesus made use of them himself,' said Miss Jones, nodding.

'Yes,' agreed Robby. 'And I think that those two angels grinned at each other and flew away, leaving Class 5a all practising being donkeys and helping each other carrying their loads.'

'Ee-yore,' agreed Miss Jones, smiling.

'Ee-yore!' said everyone else.

Four weeks later, class 5a performed their nativity play and their parents were so impressed that they could hardly stop clapping. At the end, they had to give three encores of 'The donkey song' that they had made up.

Christmas cribs

Let's make an edible stable to remind us of being a donkey!

You need:
- ☆ Several packets of any oblong-shaped plain biscuits, with enough for every child to have three biscuits, plus a few spares in case of breakages.
- ☆ Enough jelly babies for everyone to have two.
- ☆ Enough square sweets for everyone to have one (for example, chocolate-covered caramels, or square pieces of fudge).
- ☆ A good supply of thick icing, made up with icing sugar and lemon juice. This should be divided into little pots with lids (for example, cottage cheese containers)—one pot for every three children.
- ☆ Icing sugar for sprinkling and a few tea-strainers and spoons.
- ☆ One spoon or flat knife per child.
- ☆ Clear gift bags (you can get nice ones with golden stars on them), golden ribbon and pieces of stiff card to transport the stables home. You need one each of these three items per child.

Note: It is better to make the stables in a room with no carpet. Otherwise, spread out protective newspapers beforehand. If there are no more than three children to one little bowl of icing, this activity does not make very much mess and the children are extremely proud of their handiwork afterwards. It's worth it!

1. Put a little icing in the middle of one of the biscuits and place the square sweet on to it.

2. Use the other two biscuits to form a roof over the sweet. Use the icing as glue to fix the roof into place at the top where the two biscuits meet, on the sides of the sweet and on the biscuit base. It doesn't matter if the children are generous with the icing—it serves not only as glue, but also as snow!

3. Spread a little icing in front of the house and sit Mary and Joseph (the two jelly babies) on it.

4. Use a tea strainer to scatter a little fresh snow (icing sugar) over the stable.

5. Place the stable on the piece of card and leave to dry.

6. Carefully slide it into the little bag and tie up with the golden ribbon.

Make several of these little cribs beforehand so that the children have a pattern to copy.

Reproduced with permission from *Does Jesus Like Cake?* published by BRF 2003 (1 84101 319 6)

HOW TO BE A REAL STAR

I wonder if you have ever seen a very young baby? What words would you use to describe a tiny baby? What kind of things can a newborn baby do? What kind of things can God do?

What an amazing happening we celebrate at Christmas! God, the almighty creator of our world who is all-powerful, reigning in heaven, saw fit to allow Jesus, a part of himself, to come into the world as a human being—a tiny, helpless, frail little baby who cried, filled his nappy, needed food and drink and a mother's care. Have you ever thought about the enormity of that?

In the Christmas play that we heard about in the story, the angels blew open the Bible at the book of Philippians, chapter 2 and verse 3. This is what we can read there:

Don't be jealous or proud, but be humble and consider others more important than yourselves. Care about them as much as you care about yourselves and think the same way that Christ Jesus thought:

Christ was truly God. But he did not try to remain equal with God. Instead he gave up everything and became a slave, when he became like one of us. Christ was humble. He obeyed God and even died on a cross.

The Bible tells us that Jesus had every right to think highly of himself and expect the best for himself. Yet he was content to be born in the discomfort of a stable, not in the richness and luxury of a palace. He wanted to use his life to help others and be obedient to God, eventually giving up his life on the cross for the sake of all of us.

Christians believe that if we want to be followers of Jesus, then it should make a difference to the way we live our lives. The children in our story understood this when they stopped all wanting to be the stars of the play. They realized that if we really want to live like Jesus, then it's a bit like being content with the humble role of being like donkeys—unglamorous, humble, prepared to help others. The funny thing is that if we read on in Philippians, it says that as we try to love others in the way Jesus did, we will shine out in the darkness of this world like—wait for it—*stars*!

Do you want to be a star? Then you must be prepared to be a donkey first!

A SONG TO SING

I'm just a stumpy, bumpy, frumpy, grumpy,
wonky, plonky, honky-tonky donkey,
And I usually don't have much to say,
But that's not the case today.
For, a few hours ago,
By the stars' soft glow,

I watched over the birth
That will change life on earth.
And I saw the night
Bathed in heav'nly light
And the angels' song
Made me sing along.
And I still am quite unable
To see why God chose my stable—
Why exposed to every danger,
Jesus lies within my manger—
For that babe so small
Is Lord over all,
So let's sing
To the newborn king!
Oh ee-yore
Ee-yore, ee-yore, ee-yore-oria!
Worship and adore him!
Ee-yore, ee-yore, ee-yore-oria!
Worship and adore the newborn king!

TEASPOON PRAYER

Thanks: Dear God, we are looking forward to the presents we are going to get at Christmas. But those presents are just to remind us of the much greater present you gave at the first Christmas, the present of Jesus. Thank you so much that you came into our world as a baby and that you lived your life for the sake of us all.

Sorry: Sorry that we often want to grab the best for ourselves.

Please: Please help us to love others as we love ourselves.

The Donkey Song

I'm just a stumpy, bumpy, frumpy, grumpy,

wonky, plonky, honky-tonky donkey,

And I usually don't have much to say,

But that's not the case today.

For, a few hours ago,

By the stars' soft glow,

I watched over the birth

That will change life on earth.

And I saw the night

Bathed in heav'nly light

And the angels' song

Made me sing along.

And I still am quite unable

To see why God chose my stable—

Why exposed to every danger,

Jesus lies within my manger—

For that babe so small is Lord over all,

So let's sing to the newborn king!

Oh ee-yore, ee-yore, ee-yore, ee-yore-oria!

Worship and adore him!

Ee-yore, ee-yore, ee-yore-oria!

Worship and adore the newborn king!

Reproduced with permission from *Does Jesus Like Cake?* published by BRF 2003 (1 84101 319 6)

SONGS

PIANO NOTATION
AND GUITAR CHORDS

(All songs arranged by David Wilkinson)

THE DONKEY SONG

(With a swing feel)

Susanna Spanring

THE GRAPEVINE SONG

(With a swing feel)

Susanna Spanring

bove! _____ And the grapes are real - ly great, for they have no sell - by date, for

love is made to nei -ther rot nor fade.

love is made to nei -ther rot nor fade.

LIFE

(With a swing feel)

Susanna Spanring

NO ONE CAN SWITCH OFF THE LIGHT OF THE WORLD

Susanna Spanring

(With a swing feel)

REST FOR THE WEARY

Prayerfully

Susanna Spanring

Note: The second half of this song (from 'Rest for the weary...') can be sung at the same time as the first half, as a descant.

THE SNOOZE SONG

(With a swing feel)

Susanna Spanring

SORRY

(With a swing feel)

Susanna Spanring

S. O. R. R. Y. Sor-ry can be hard to say. But once it's heard, that lit-tle ti-ny word can clear a lot of trou-ble a-way. It may take grit to come out with it but sor-ry real-ly makes your day... Sor-ry, sor-ry, sor-ry, as the sun goes down, let me try a smile and wipe off the frown. Sor-ry, sor-ry, sor-ry, let's for-get our fight and live our lives as chil-dren of the light.

★ ★ ★ ★ ★ ★ ★

OTHER RESOURCES FROM BARNABAS

step into the

STORY

20 story and activity sessions for creative learning

Margaret Spivey and Anna Jean

☆ Ideal for 6–10s ☆ Includes photocopy permission ☆

REF 1 84101 002 2, £15.99

This book offers an imaginative and vibrant approach to the message and story of the Bible. Each unit begins with a retelling of a selected story, designed to be read aloud in assemblies, classrooms, church groups or family services. It then explores the story in depth through the five senses—sight, sound, touch, taste and smell—using practical exercises to bring the story alive.

Each section concludes with ideas for imaginative prayer. The material is ideal for all those wishing to explore spiritual awareness with primary aged children and bridges the gap between word and understanding for non-book pupils.

★ ★ ★ ★ ★ ★ ★

OTHER RESOURCES
FROM BARNABAS

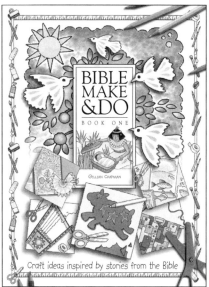

REF 1 84101 332 3, £5.99

Book 1 includes creation, Joseph's coat, Moses in the bulrushes, David's harp, Jonah, the Christmas story, the centurion's servant, the storm on the lake, the lost sheep and Jesus enters Jerusalem.

Book 2 includes Noah's ark, God's promises to Abraham, Jacob and Esau, Gideon's victory, Daniel in the lion's den, wise men's gifts, loaves and fishes, the wise and foolish girls, the lost coin and Jesus is alive!

REF 1 84101 333 1, £5.99

Book 3 includes Rebecca's kindness, Joseph's dreams, The plagues of Egypt, The golden lampstand, David and Goliath, Jesus is born, Jesus is baptized, The wedding at Cana, Peter lets Jesus down, and Pentecost.

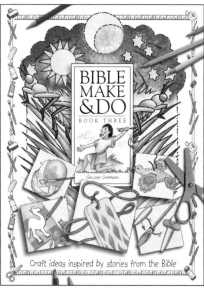

REF 1 84101 344 7, £5.99

Book 4 includes The tower of Babel, Joseph interprets dreams, Moses crosses the Red Sea, The strength of Samson, The shepherd's surprise, The good seed, The prodigal son, The first Easter, Peter's chains, and The hidden treasure.

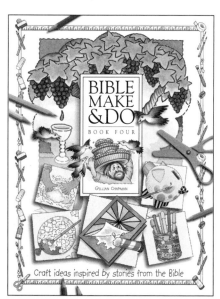

REF 1 84101 345 5, £5.99

Familiar stories from the Bible with practical craft ideas. Each double-page project spread features a retelling of the Bible story, followed by instructions for a craft to bring the story to life. Cutting guides are also included.

Craft ideas include collage, papier mâché modelling, print-making and weaving using inexpensive materials and equipment with emphasis on recycling and using everyday materials wherever possible.

Specific projects, such as masks, costume accessories and artefacts, can also be used as props for drama productions.

Visit the brf website www.brf.org.uk

BARNABAS RESOURCES INFORMATION

Please keep me informed about new Barnabas services and resources.

Rev/Dr/Mr/Mrs/Miss _____

Address _____

_____ Post Code _____

Telephone _____ Fax _____

E-mail _____

Do you have responsibilities in any of the following areas?

Sunday School .... ❏   Teacher.. ❏

Children's Club .... ❏   *Which age group?*

Which age range?   *Reception* .... ❏

3-5 .... ❏   *KS1*.. ❏

5-7 .... ❏   *KS2*.. ❏

7-11 .... ❏   Educational Adviser/Consultant .... ❏

8-12 .... ❏   Church Children's Work Adviser .... ❏

Other (please specify) _____

Please send me

❏   Annual Barnabas Catalogue

Please send me information about

❏   Seasonal resources

❏   Teaching resources for children

❏   Leadership resources

❏   Barnabas Live for schools

❏   Inset training

❏   Training for local church children's leaders

❏   Bible Unplugged events for children

❏   I would like to support Barnabas ministry with a donation

Data Protection Notice
Under the new Data Protection Act legislation BRF must obtain your consent to hold and use information about you. Please sign below to confirm your consent.

   BRF will use the information supplied above to fulfil your orders, and to service your requests for further information. The information will be stored both electronically on computer and in a manual filing system until you inform us otherwise. It may be used to inform you of other BRF products, activities and services. BRF will not supply your details to any other companies other than to fulfil orders from BRF.
I confirm my consent to the Data Protection Notice above.

Signed: _____

PLEASE RETURN THIS FORM TO: BRF, FREEPOST (OF758), OXFORD, OX2 8YY

First Floor, Elsfield Hall, 15 - 17 Elsfield Way, Oxford OX2 8FG
Tel: 01865 319700] Fax: 01865 319701] Email: enquiries@brf.org.uk
Charity No. 233280] VAT No. GB 238 5574 35

www.brf.org.uk

Enter an author, title, subject or phrase

Books ○
Extracts/Info ●

go

brf

● **Resourcing your spiritual journey** ●

barnabas

Home
Bible Centre
Book news
Events
Articles
Authors
Who is BRF?

**The Bible Reading
Fellowship**
First Floor
Elsfield Hall
15–17 Elsfield Way
Oxford
OX2 8FG
England
Tel 01865 319700
Fax 01865 319701
E-mail
enquiries@brf.org.uk

Welcome to BRF

For Bible based resources and information for today's Christian living and for details of all BRF publications, extracts and articles, and a wealth of other information.

Find out about:

■ New BRF publications

■ BRF's comprehensive range of resources:
Bible reading and study; Prayer and spirituality; Lent and Advent

■ BRF authors

■ Quiet days, Retreats and other events

■ Barnabas (storybooks, seasonal activity books and teaching resources for 3–11 year olds)

■ The Barnabas Live Creative Arts and Schools Programme

Visit the BRF website at www.brf.org.uk

BRF is a Registered Charity